a PIRATE'S LIFE

for SHE

a PIRATE'S
LIFE for SHE

swashbuckling
women
through the ages

LAURA SOOK DUNCOMBE

CHICAGO
REVIEW
PRESS

Copyright © 2020 by Laura Sook Duncombe
All rights reserved
Published by Chicago Review Press Incorporated
814 North Franklin Street
Chicago, Illinois 60610
ISBN 978-1-64160-055-2

Library of Congress Cataloging-in-Publication Data
Is available from the Library of Congress

Interior design: Jonathan Hahn
Table of contents illustrations: Natalya Balnova

Printed in the United States of America
5 4 3 2 1

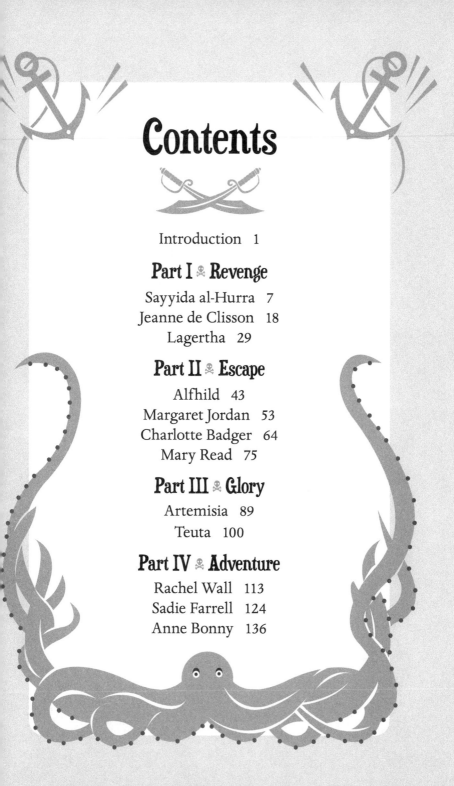

Contents

Part V ☠ Power

Introduction

A pirate is no master of disguise. The eye patch, the peg leg, the parrot, the big feathered hat—all of these things are very conspicuous. Even a person who has never met a pirate can identify one by sight. But is it just as easy to identify who a pirate *is*, instead of just how a pirate *looks*?

In reality, pirates are so much more (and so much harder to define) than their costumes. It is nearly impossible to find a common trait that applies to all pirates. Not time: they have sailed throughout every millennium. Not location: they hail from every inhabited continent. Not age, color, or creed either. Not even gender can be used to identify a pirate, for there have been male and female pirates since piracy began.

Female pirates have sailed alongside, or in some instances in command of, their male counterparts since ancient times. Yet for most of recorded history, their stories have been kept out of pirate books. Male historians have ignored female pirates, essentially saying the women's stories do not matter. Even today, women are sometimes told their experiences do not matter. But all women's stories *do* matter. They deserve to be told just as much the stories of men, which have dominated the conversation for so long.

Men's stories occupy a well-established place in our imaginations and on our bookshelves. These histories are not being erased; they are simply being asked to make room for others' experiences. When men cannot or will not share their space, women must demand it, or take it. The pirates in this book have a lot to teach women today about taking things that other people say they cannot have. For there to be equality, the truth must be told. The truth is that women pirates have existed, do exist, and will continue to exist as long as there is a sea to sail upon.

Pirates are, first and foremost, criminals. It may seem strange to celebrate the lives of women who stole, tortured, and even killed for a living. However, pirates captivate readers despite their bad behavior. The women in this book gave up home and comfort for a chance to live outside society's rules and experience true freedom. That desire to be free—free from society, free from gender roles, and free from a life mapped out before it has begun—is something many people identify with. It is possible to admire these women's courage, confidence, power, and intelligence without approving of their illegal actions. No person is entirely good or entirely bad, and there is plenty of good to appreciate in these "bad" women.

The stories in this book are divided into five parts. Each part explores a different reason women practiced piracy: revenge, escape, glory, adventure, and power. The women in each section share few similarities besides their motivation. In fact, the 16 women profiled in this book have little in common. They include old women, young women, poor women, rich women, mothers, daughters, religious women, atheist women, queens, and peasants. They pirated from 500 BCE to today. They come from Asia, Africa, Europe, North America, and the Caribbean. Some of them would not even recognize the form of pirating that others practice. Yet they are united. Each woman looked at the life that lay before her, saw what society told her a woman was allowed to have, and said, "No, thanks!" Each woman dreamed of controlling her own destiny. In becoming pirates, these women wrote their own stories instead of acting out the stories someone else wrote for them.

Readers should understand that it is difficult to separate fact from legend in pirate history. Pirates were, by their very nature, often not part of the official records of their day. Because they lived beyond the reach of the law, their stories were not recorded in conventional ways. However, these stories do not deserve to be cast into the trash can of history just because we cannot verify every fact. After all, how can a reader ever totally verify the truthfulness of a past event when two books written on the subject might say completely different things? History can change dramatically depending on who is doing the telling. As Keith Jenkins says in *Re-thinking History*, "the past and history are two separate things." That being said, every effort has been made to include only the most accurate information in this book.

Prepare to set sail with the most cutthroat women who ever sailed the seven seas! I am so excited for you to meet these women whom I love so much. I hope their stories will amaze you, surprise you, and, most of all, inspire you. After all, you are the next generation of adventurers. What brilliant discoveries will you make, and what radical actions will you take, with these bold and daring women as your guides?

Laura Sook Duncombe
Tulsa, Oklahoma
August 7, 2018

Part I
REVENGE

Sayyida al-Hurra

When Catholic monarchs King Ferdinand of Castile and Queen Isabella of Aragon pushed the Muslims out of Spain in 1492, they radically changed the lives of many people. An entire population of men, women, and children became refugees, forced to either give up their religion or leave their homes.

One of these refugees, just a child during her family's flight from Granada, never forgot what Ferdinand and Isabella did to her family. When she grew up, she made Europe pay for the monarchs' crimes. Ferdinand and Isabella might not have suspected that their actions would give birth to a powerful pirate with a bone-deep need for revenge, but they should have realized that the world's history is a house of cards—shake one card and the entire tower quakes. Their Reconquista (a Spanish and Portuguese word that means "reconquest") was the shake that created Sayyida al-Hurra, a Muslim ruler and undisputed pirate queen of the Mediterranean Sea.

Sayyida was born sometime around 1485 in Granada. Today, Granada is part of Andalusia, Spain, but at the time of Sayyida's birth, it was an emirate, or kingdom, ruled by Muslim rulers called emirs. In 1492, after a long fight, Catholic monarchs Ferdinand and Isabella took complete control of the Iberian Peninsula, which includes Granada, and forced all Muslims to convert to Christianity or flee. Sayyida's family, an elite and wealthy Muslim family called the Banu Rashid, chose to flee.

Even though Sayyida is a famous pirate, nobody knows her real name. *Sayyida al-Hurra* is actually a title, an Arabic phrase that loosely translates to "independent noble lady" or "female sovereign." Some sources claim her birth name was Aisha, which means "lively woman."

The title she wore definitely fit her personality. Although she was very young when her family left Granada and became refugees, she probably had memories of the land of her birth and the life her family enjoyed there. She deeply resented her family's forced evacuation and refused to let the people who were responsible get away with it.

She spent the rest of her childhood in Chaouen, Morocco, where her family eventually settled. Morocco, along with many other parts of North Africa, was a place where many Muslim transplants created homes and businesses. Sayyida's father was instrumental in establishing their new hometown as a place where all refugees were welcome.

THE RECONQUISTA

The Granada War, which ended Muslim rule on the Iberian Peninsula, was part of a large campaign to retake formerly Christian lands from their Muslim rulers and return them to the Christian rule that they had experienced under the Visigoths (a nomadic group of Germanic people who flourished in late antiquity). It was not one long war but a series of battles from 711 to 1492 CE. Many rulers of various nations were a part of this re-Christianization, or Reconquista, including King Charlemagne.

In the beginning, these battles were seen as a land conquest, not a holy war. Before the Reconquista, Muslims and Christians from this area often allied with each other in battles with other Muslim and Christian kingdoms. Some people, called mercenaries, fought for whichever side paid the most, regardless of religion. The two religions were not always sworn enemies. With its Crusades in the Middle Ages, the Catholic church changed the focus of these battles from landowner versus landowner to Christians versus "infidels." Sadly, Christian bias against Muslims lingers to this day in many parts of the world.

Because Sayyida came from a wealthy family, she was tutored at home. She did well in all subjects and was especially good at languages. It seemed obvious to everyone who knew her that she would become an important woman someday.

Sayyida's life in Chaouen was a happy one. Her education was longer and more extensive than that of most other girls in her time. But like all girls of this era—rich or poor—after her studies were over, it was time for her to get married and have a family. When she was a child, Sayyida had been promised in marriage to a friend of the family. Her betrothed, Abu Al-Hasan al-Mandri, was the governor of a neighboring town, Tétouan. With many ships coming in and out of it daily, Tétouan was a major seaport in the area. It had been sacked by the Portuguese in 1400 and was a shadow of its former self, but al-Mandri saw potential in the neglected city, which the sultan gave him as a refugee city. He had a dream to make Tétouan great again, and he knew his new bride could help him. Although they did not marry for love and al-Mandri was a great deal older than Sayyida, the two were a strong match. He valued her opinion and respected her.

Once they were married, Sayyida did help al-Mandri in his quest to make Tétouan a thriving town. She shared the duties of ruling with her husband and was regarded by their people as a leader. The al-Mandris painstakingly restored Tétouan to its former glory and turned it into a bustling metropolis featuring a Great Mosque and narrow, mazelike streets designed to confuse intruders. Today, old town Tétouan is a United Nations Educational, Scientific and Cultural Organization (UNESCO)

World Heritage site, in no small part because of the work completed by Sayyida and her husband.

After her husband died in 1515, Sayyida ruled Tét-ouan by herself. She officially became Sayyida al-Hurra, hakimat titwan (sovereign lady, governor of Tétouan). Historians believe she was the last Islamic woman to claim the title of *al-Hurra,* which means "free woman" and was traditionally given to a woman with great power. For about 25 years, Sayyida governed her new hometown alone, bringing the formerly abandoned city to new heights of wealth. She accomplished this great feat using two very different methods. First, she elevated Tétouan with the business and diplomatic skills she honed over a quarter century of governing. Second, she expanded Tétouan through an alliance with the notori-ous Barbarossa brothers—a family of pirates.

~~~~~~~~~~~~~~~~~~~~~~~~

THE BARBAROSSA

Few names struck fear into a person's heart like the Barbary corsairs, and the most famous and feared of all the corsairs were the Barbarossa. Many legends explain where the family got the name Barbarossa, from one brother's red beard to a translation of "Uncle Oruç," but nobody knows for sure why they were called that. It was not the family's last name.

Oruç and Khizr Reis were born on the island of Les-bos to a Grecian mother and a Turkish father. They started their careers as sailors and eventually became privateers for Turkey. Oruç was captured by Christians and enslaved for three years before eventually gaining his freedom. When he returned home, he and his brother returned to privateering and made their home island of Lesbos a base for privateers.

The brothers moved to the Barbary Coast in the early 1500s and immediately started raiding Christian-controlled seaports and coastal villages from there with great success. They rose to the top of the corsairs and became leaders—Oruç eventually became sultan of Algiers. When Oruç was killed in 1518, Khizr took over the operation and joined forces with Suleiman the Magnificent, sultan of the Ottoman Empire. The sultan gave Khizr the title *Khair-ed-din*, which means "best of the religion."

Khizr became an even better pirate than his brother had been and did much to ensure that the name Barbarossa would be known throughout history. Khizr had a long and illustrious career as a corsair as well as a statesman and died in 1546. At his death, Turkish records proclaimed that "the King of the Sea is dead."

By the time Sayyida reached out to the pirates, the younger brother, Khizr, was in charge, running the operation from Algiers. Although nearly 500 miles separated Tétouan from Khair-ed-din's headquarters, somehow Sayyida contacted the corsair king and obtained a blessing to go into privateering, as well as some information on how to do it. What could have inspired Sayyida to reach out to fearsome pirates? How was the famous pirate swayed by Sayyida? The world may never know. With Khizr's blessing, Sayyida began her privateering career and quickly became the "undisputed leader of the pirates in the western Mediterranean," according to scholar Fatima Mernissi.

Sayyida and the Barbarossa controlled the entire Mediterranean Sea—Sayyida the western part and the Barbarossa the eastern part. In fact, the Western world knows about Sayyida from her appearances in the logs of the Spanish and Portuguese ships that were attacked by her or forced to negotiate with her. She became the person to talk to if a hostage needed to be released or an embargo needed to be lifted. Simply put, if you had business of any kind in the western Mediterranean Sea, you had business with Sayyida.

So how did the pirates take control of the Mediterranean? Two ways: their ships and their reputation. The pirates' ships, galliots, were modified galley ships. Galleys were long, slender warships primarily powered by rowing, although they also had sails. Galliots were smaller and faster than traditional galleys, which gave them a big advantage over the Spanish and Portuguese ships they attacked. A pirate ship could never outfire a better armed military or merchant ship, so it had to outmaneuver them. Corsairs usually sailed up behind an enemy's ship and boarded it from the rear, surprising the crew. Because they usually attacked merchant ships with few fighting men aboard, as opposed to military ships full of soldiers, the hand-to-hand battles were often short and went in the corsairs' favor.

BARBARY CORSAIRS AND SLAVERY

Pirate stories frequently feature cruel behavior and ferocious appetites, but the stories of the Barbary corsairs are among the darkest. The corsairs made entire villages vanish in the dead of night. Legends in their own time, they were feared by children and adults alike. Most of the outrage surrounding the corsairs stems from the fact that they regularly kidnapped and enslaved Christians. The Western world did not take kindly to the idea of Muslim corsairs enslaving Christians, ignoring the fact that a vast number of the Barbary corsairs were not native Muslims but in fact *renegadoes*, European-born Christians who joined the Barbary ranks to take part in the more exciting pirating happening in the Mediterranean.

The truth is that corsairs did routinely enslave Christian men, women, and children. However, European Christians at this time were also enslaving Muslims. Historian Salvatore Bono has suggested that there were roughly as many Islamic slaves in early Christendom as there were Christian slaves in early Islamdom. The elder Barbarossa brother himself was enslaved by a Christian order of knights. So, slavery alone did not merit the Barbary pirates' monstrous reputation. Given that most early Western sources on Barbary corsairs were written by Christians, it is possible that Islamophobia (and the desire for Muslim-held land) caused the Barbary reputation for cruelty to be exaggerated.

Even if a ship did have trained fighters, the widespread, fearsome reputation of the Barbary corsairs made all but the bravest of men surrender quickly. The stories about the ruthless Barbary pirates, mostly exaggerated xenophobia, did a lot of the corsairs' work for them. Because people were so afraid of the Barbary pirates, they gave up without a fight, basically handing over their treasure. After the crew was subdued, the corsairs would strip the ship of any valuable cargo: mostly gold, supplies, and slaves.

Sayyida's piratical work didn't just revitalize her town, it repaid the Spanish for kicking the Muslims out of Granada. Time had passed, but the wounds had not healed, nor had her desire for revenge cooled. Sayyida made sure that the Spanish knew they were not forgiven for what they had done, and that she would make them pay for it. She built her town into a successful new home, but she did it with money stolen from those who had stolen from her. Her success must have felt doubly sweet— she did not just help her own people but also hurt those who had hurt her.

Sayyida had, by her mid-40s, accomplished a successful political and piratical career. But she had one more achievement in her, one that would gain her a special footnote in the history books. During a tour of his kingdom in 1541, Sultan Abu al-Abbas Ahmad ibn Muhammad of the Wattasid dynasty met Sayyida in Tétouan. The king of Fez was so taken with her that he immediately proposed marriage. Sayyida accepted his proposal but refused to make the 170-mile journey to Fez for the wedding, insisting that it take place in Tétouan instead. The sultan, astonishingly, agreed to this demand and traveled to her instead. The pair was married in Tétouan—the only time in Moroccan history that a king was married outside his capital city. On her wedding day, the sultan's bride to be might have reflected on how far she had come, or maybe she dreamed of what she still hoped to do.

Despite her new status as wife of a sultan, Sayyida was not destined to rule much longer. Her son-in-law from her first marriage, Moulay al-Mandri, became involved in the inter-dynasty warfare of the region. He sensed that the political tide was turning and that his mother-in-law's new husband was not going to remain in power for much longer. He believed it was in his own best interest to sever ties with the Wattasids and join the rival Saadis instead. (It turned out that he was right. The sultan was captured by the Saadis in 1545, and the Wattasid dynasty ceased to exist nine years after that, in 1554.) In 1542, Moulay arrived in Tétouan with an army, ready to remove Sayyida from power, forcibly if necessary. Sayyida stepped down, and just like that, her

40-year career as governor, pirate, and sultana was over. Exactly what happened to her afterward is unknown. Most sources say she returned home to Chaouen, where she retired and lived peacefully until her death.

Sayyida went into the pirating business for revenge, but she was also a brilliant woman who used her skills to make her new home country a better place. Her methods were unorthodox, but she did what had to be done to revitalize Tétouan.

Learn More

Abulafia, David. *The Great Sea: The Human History of the Mediterranean*. Oxford: Oxford University Press, 2011.

Konstam, Angus. *Piracy: The Complete History*. Oxford: General Military, 2008.

Mernissi, Fatima. *Forgotten Queens of Islam*. Minneapolis: University of Minnesota Press, 1993.

Peirce, Leslie. *The Imperial Harem: Women and Sovereignty in the Ottoman Empire*. Oxford: Oxford University Press, 1993.

Wilson, Peter Lamborn. *Pirate Utopias: Moorish Corsairs and European Renegadoes*. 2nd ed. Brooklyn: Autonomedia, 2003.

Jeanne de Clisson

Since the beginning of time, wars have been waged primarily by men. In the past, men ordered other men to go fight, and women and children stayed behind with no say in the matter. Women were forced to wait and pray, hoping that the men they loved—brothers, fathers, husbands, and more—would not pay the ultimate price for another man's decision.

One woman, Jeanne de Clisson, decided that she was through living in a world where men could kill other men during war and get away with it. When a man she loved was killed, she killed back. Her quest for revenge earned her the nickname the Lioness of Brittany.

Jeanne was born Jeanne de Belleville sometime around 1300. Historians say she was one of the most beautiful women of her day. Her parents were wealthy nobles, and she grew up in the family castle called

Belleville-sur-Vie. The castle and fortress were on the western coast of France, around 170 miles from Brittany. Jeanne enjoyed a peaceful childhood. As the young girl played on her family's estate and visited the beaches in summer, she had no idea how important the faraway province of Brittany would become to her in just a few years.

Jeanne later married a Breton nobleman, and the couple had two children before he died in 1326. Four years later, Jeanne married Olivier de Clisson. He was a very wealthy nobleman from Brittany who owned large estates all over France and Brittany. It is unknown how they met, but Jeanne and Olivier seem to have married for love, which was very rare in that time.

The Clissons had five children together. They lived a happy, mostly uneventful life at their many homes across western France until the War of Breton Succession broke out. That was the beginning of the end of the Clisson family's life as they knew it.

WAR OF BRETON SUCCESSION

Brittany, now part of western France, was once its own state. In the Middle Ages, it was ruled by a duke. The people of Brittany are called Bretons, and although in Jeanne's time some were loyal to England and some to France, most Bretons felt that they were Breton above all. They had their own language and culture separate from both of the other countries, and they took great pride in having their own rulers.

Naturally, both France and England sought Brittany as their ally. They were very invested in who was on the ducal throne in Brittany, because his allegiance would be a huge benefit to whichever country he chose. So, when John III, Duke of Brittany, died childless in 1341 and the line of succession was thrown into doubt, a war erupted in Brittany. This war lasted for over 20 years and played a major part in the foundation of the Hundred Years' War. The two sides of the war were the French-backed House Blois, who claimed John III's niece Joan was the rightful heir, and House Montfort, who claimed John III's half-brother, also named John, belonged on the throne. The English-backed Montfort eventually won the duchy and kept it in his family for almost 200 years.

When the war began, Olivier and Jeanne backed the French candidate for duke, Joan de Penthiévre, and her husband, Charles de Blois. Charles and Olivier were old friends, so it made sense that the Clissons would take Charles's side. Olivier fought for some time without incident, but during the battle for Vannes (a Breton city) in 1342, Olivier was taken prisoner by the English.

Charles was horrified that his friend had been taken prisoner, and he offered to pay any amount of ransom to ensure Olivier's freedom. The English asked for what seemed to Charles to be a suspiciously small amount of money for Olivier. This act planted a seed in Charles's mind that Olivier had not defended Vannes as strongly as he could have. Maybe Olivier was not as loyal to House Blois as he claimed.

Over time, Charles became convinced that Olivier was a traitor to the French cause and House Blois. Whether or not Olivier actually betrayed Charles is unknown, but there is no evidence to suggest he had been anything other than a true friend.

In 1343, a truce (which turned out to be temporary) was signed between England and France. Charles used the truce as an opportunity to get rid of his perceived enemy, Olivier. Charles enlisted the help of King Philip VI for this dark deed. The plan was to send Olivier and a few other Breton lords an invitation to France. The invitations advertised a friendly sports tournament to celebrate the truce. Olivier packed his bags and went to France, probably looking forward to seeing his friend Charles and enjoying some leisure time. When Olivier arrived in France, he was shocked to find no tournament. Instead, soldiers took him prisoner and accused him of treason. He was quickly put on trial, convicted, and beheaded. His severed head was displayed publicly on a pike as proof of France's might and a warning to anyone who might want to change allegiances and betray France.

Olivier's beheading (and the display of his head) sent shock waves through the Breton upper class. The entire affair was highly unusual, and many parts of it struck people as suspicious. For instance, no evidence had been presented at trial to prove Olivier's guilt, other than the statement that he had confessed to the crime. Furthermore, it was rare for a person of Olivier's standing to be beheaded and put on display. This type of punishment was usually reserved for low-class or common criminals. Some people thought that King Philip VI had been over-zealous, to say the least, in convicting Olivier in such a way. Some even thought that the king had killed an innocent man. One of those people was Olivier's widow, Jeanne.

When Jeanne heard about her husband's murder, her life changed forever. She had lost the man she loved, and her provider. She could not remain in her castle and take solace in her children—King Philip VI confiscated much of the family's property after the murder. Without an income, a husband, or even a home, she was forced to choose a different path for herself and her children. She chose piracy and revenge for her husband's death.

The first thing Jeanne did was take her children to Nantes to see their father's severed head. Jeanne wanted her children to understand the injustice that their family was up against. More important, she wanted them to hate the French as passionately as she now did. If Jeanne had to explain to her children why they had to say good-bye to their home and their way of life, she could hardly have asked for a more dramatic reason than the severed head of their father. After the viewing, Jeanne cut all ties with House Blois and the French and vowed to make them pay for what they had taken from her family. She would start her own personal war, and she would begin close to home.

Jeanne's first act of war was to sack a nearby fort. She and a small band of men loyal to her cause asked the guards to open the gate. Recognizing Jeanne as a neighbor, the guards let her in without any trouble. Once inside, Jeanne and her men wrought destruction on people and property alike, leaving only one man alive to tell the story of what he'd seen and to spread the message Jeanne had instructed him to share. The message was this: Jeanne de Clisson was coming for France, and no one was safe from her vengeance.

Financing her war was not easy. It was difficult for Jeanne to raise an army because most of her land and possessions had been confiscated by the French king as part of her husband's sentence. But Jeanne persevered through the hardship; she sold her remaining fine jewels and anything else she could sell and put together a seaworthy fighting force that terrorized French ships anywhere they found them.

Jeanne's first act as shipowner was to paint the hulls black and dye the sails blood red. She clearly was not interested in maintaining a low profile. She wanted her ships to be instantly recognizable so her enemies would know exactly who was coming for them. The battle plan was simple: attack viciously and leave only one survivor to spread the word. As might be expected, the word did get around. French people everywhere were afraid of the ruthless Jeanne de Clisson. No one knew where she might strike next.

One story comes up repeatedly in legends about Jeanne, although it has not yet been proven. It is said that France's King Philip VI himself was forced to join the fight to stop Jeanne, due to her ruthless effectiveness. He sent ships to attack her, and for once, Jeanne was the one taken by surprise. The battle was long and bloody, and Jeanne barely managed to escape alive. She and her children were stranded miles from the shore in a small rowboat with nothing but the clothes on their backs.

A weaker woman might have admitted defeat at that moment, but Jeanne would never give in until she won justice for Olivier. She was realistic about her prospects. She knew that to survive and have a chance of reentering the fight after this catastrophic battle, she would have to do something drastic. In that little rowboat, Jeanne made a plan that was so harebrained it was almost impossible. She and her children would row all the way to England and appeal directly to the English king for help.

Historical documents prove that Jeanne was, at one time, on the English payroll. The English king may have even helped her buy her fleet of black ships. So the story about rowing to England might be true, or Jeanne could have come into contact with the English in some other way. Whatever her relationship with England, it seems she was only interested in helping England because doing so meant hurting France. If the English profited, lucky for them, but Jeanne fought, first and foremost, to avenge her husband.

Jeanne and her black fleet sailed up and down the English Channel, laying waste to every French vessel in their path. The Lioness of Brittany continued to strike fear into the hearts of French sailors everywhere, and she did a considerable amount of damage during the black fleet years.

~~~~~~~~~~~~~~~~~~~~~~~~~~~~~~~~~~~~~~~

WOMEN IN THE MIDDLE AGES

In the Middle Ages, the life of the average woman in in Europe was very different than the life of Western women today. Women typically had one of only three careers: housewife, midwife, or nun. Most women, whether rich or poor, stayed home, had children, and managed their households. Childbirth was a great killer of women in this period: approximately 20 percent of women died either during childbirth or from complications after childbirth. Life expectancy was not long, and lives were generally not filled with leisure or comfort.

One of the safest places a woman could be during the Middle Ages was in a religious order. Nuns did not marry and generally did not have to worry about death in childbirth. In the convent, they had access to some simple education—more than the average housewife did. Also, women in the church were able to advance through the ranks of nuns, from postulant all the way up to mother superior. It was perhaps the only job at that time offering women the opportunity to advance. Other than a queen, no woman was more powerful than a mother superior.

~~~~~~~~~~~~~~~~~~~~~~~~~~~~~~~~~~~~~~~

France's King Philip VI died in 1350, but Jeanne's pirating career lived on. She continued to sail and destroy any French ship that got in her way. No one can say what motivated her to keep fighting the French after her major enemy—her husband's murderer—was dead. Maybe she remained in the fight to ensure that her new choice for the duchy, John de Montfort, safely ascended to the throne. However, Jeanne retired some eight years before the conflict came to an end and Montfort's position was secure. What was she waiting for, if it was neither the death of the king nor the coronation of the duke? The answer is unknown. Regardless of why her piratical career lasted as long as it did, by the time she retired from piracy she had captured enough ships and killed enough men to claim a spot in pirate history.

In 1356, Jeanne traded in her sword and pants for a wedding dress when she married Sir Walter Bentley, a deputy of King Edward III of England. How they met and why they married, like so much of Jeanne's life, is a mystery. Once they wed, the couple settled in Brittany in a property given to Walter by Edward III. Their new home was called Hennebont Castle. As luck would have it, before it was owned by the Bentleys, it had been the site of a famous battle won by another female pirate also named Jeanne: Jeanne de Montfort.

Jeanne de Clisson died sometime around 1359, knowing that she had won all her battles. She could not have predicted that her son, Olivier, childhood friend of the duke of Brittany John de Montfort, would eventually

JEANNE DE MONTFORT

The War of Breton Succession boasts not one but two female warriors, both named Jeanne. While Jeanne de Clisson first fought for the French and eventually sided with the English, Jeanne de Montfort was always in the English camp. Her husband, John de Montfort, had a claim to the ducal throne and was the English choice for it. Jeanne was said to have "the courage of the man and the heart of a lion." Her story possibly inspired another Jeanne—young Jeanne d'Arc—to fight for her country.

Jeanne and her husband were opposed by King Philip VI of France. They decided to rule Brittany anyway, acting as if they were already the duke and duchess. Their actions gained popular support, but Philip VI did not approve. The Montforts were forced to flee France or risk capture, imprisonment, or worse.

Despite their efforts, Charles de Blois captured John de Montfort and imprisoned him in a tower at the Louvre in Paris. Once her husband was in jail, Jeanne wholeheartedly took up the cause, leading her family's troops into battle. She was called "the flame" because she personally set her enemy's camp on fire during the siege on Hennebont Castle. She fought on land and sea, even after her husband was killed in battle. Her son John was eventually given the ducal throne, in large part due to her efforts; he in turn passed the title to his own son.

switch sides again and fight for the French. He was a fearsome soldier who earned the nickname the Butcher. Jeanne's quest for vengeance against the French did not live on with Olivier Jr., but her determination to fight for what she desired—and her violent, bloodthirsty methods—definitely were passed down to her son.

Learn More

Gosse, Phillip. *The History of Piracy*. Lt. ed. Mineola, NY: Dover, 2007.

Klausmann, Ulrike, et al. *Women Pirates and the Politics of the Jolly Roger*, trans. Nicholas Levis. Montreal: Black Rose Books, 1997.

Taylor, Craig. "The Salic Law, French Queenship, and the Defense of Women in the Late Middle Ages." *French Historical Studies* 29, no. 4 (Fall 2006): 543–564.

Lagertha

Women have not always been able to make their own choices. Sometimes choices were made for them that placed them into unfamiliar situations they never could have anticipated. One woman who found herself in a situation like this, and decided to make her own choices in response, was named Lagertha. The main account of her story comes from the *Gesta Danorum*, a history of the Danish people written in the 12th century by Saxo Grammaticus. Her desire to make someone pay for the indignities she had been forced to suffer led her to piracy.

To call Lagertha a pirate may be a bit of a stretch, but she did engage in naval warfare, so she is often lumped into the pirate category by historians. Also, Vikings pioneered some seafaring methods that were copied by later pirates. According to historian Jo Stanley, for female Vikings, "to conquer enemies, to defeat others, could be seen as theft: of their lives, their ships, and their right to fight for a cause." Since pirates are masters of theft, it is reasonable to call Viking women pirates. If not technically pirates in name, Vikings are definitely pirates in spirit.

This particular Viking pirate is known by many names. Lagertha is also called Ladgerda, Hlathgerth, and Thorgerd. Sometimes she is described as a goddess and other times as a mortal woman. Whoever she was, Lagertha entered history as a family member of a Norwegian king, Siward. King Frey of Sweden attacked King Siward, killed him, and put the women of his household into a brothel. He did this solely to humiliate the dead king—the women's humiliation was not considered.

Lagertha was one of the women forced into sexual slavery. She would not stay there for long, though; she and some of the other women somehow cobbled together makeshift weapons and planned to fight their way to freedom. They were getting out of the brothel, no matter what. Saxo Grammaticus says these women preferred "death to outrage."

Ragnar Lodbrok, the Danish king and grandson of the slain King Siward, was horrified to hear of the treatment of these women, many of them his kinsfolk. Whether because of a sense of family duty or decency, or perhaps even a desire to expand his territory, Ragnar decided to invade the enemy Frey's kingdom and liberate

~~~~~~

WOMEN AS COLLATERAL

Although wars are not usually waged by women, it is often women who bear the consequences. Just like in Lagertha's story, women all over the world are kidnapped, tortured, and killed by invading armies to subdue their enemies. It is not an accidental part of war but a tactic of war, used knowingly by men.

From ancient times to the present day, this has happened and is still happening. The United Nations has strict rules forbidding the practice of using the pain of women to demoralize men during war, but it happens anyway and often goes unpunished. Organizations such as Amnesty International investigate and keep statistics on this problem, and it does not appear to be getting any better. Lagertha took up a sword and fought her way out, but many women are not able to do the same. When a war is proposed, leaders must take into account the lives that will be lost, not just the lives of soldiers, but also of women and children bystanders. Leaders who do not learn this lesson doom the women under their care to trauma and even death.

~~~~~~

the women from the brothel. No doubt he expected to be greeted as a hero by the grateful women. Instead, he was met by armed warriors who joined him on the battlefield. During the furious battle that followed, one woman "fought in front among the bravest with her hair loose over her shoulders," and caught the eye of Ragnar. Everyone on the battlefield noticed this powerful warrior woman, who slew her every opponent and was not bothered in the slightest by the carnage around her.

Finally, with the women's help, the battle was won. Now that vengeance was secured and the women were all freed, Ragnar was determined to find the identity of the mystery warrior woman, the one who caused him to "gain the victory by the might of just one woman." It didn't take long to discover that the strong fighter was Lagertha. Armed with this knowledge, Ragnar set out to woo Lagertha and win her as his wife.

Possibly because she had just escaped from a brothel, Lagertha was not too keen on marrying anyone, Ragnar included. She guarded her quarters with a hound and a bear to keep unwanted visitors away. But Ragnar was not put off by the wild animals. He wanted Lagertha for his wife, and he would have her no matter how she felt about it. He snuck up on her home, stabbed the bear, and choked the dog. With her guardians out of the way, Lagertha had no choice but to marry her "rescuer" Ragnar. The couple eventually wed and had three children, and all was apparently well for several years.

Their wedded bliss was not to last. Ragnar returned to his native Denmark to maintain his hold on the throne, leaving his wife and children in Norway. Denmark had a number of warring factions that wanted to rule the country, and Ragnar was constantly under attack for his title. While he was away from Lagertha, his amorous attentions began to shift to another woman. Saxo notes that

VIKING LONGSHIPS

A Viking's longship was not just her means of transportation, it was her entire life. Without a ship, a Viking could accomplish nothing. So, what were these ships like? They were approximately 100 feet long with lean wooden hulls (bodies). The masts were often covered in gold, and the sails were made of fine silks sewn together with golden thread. The ropes, called rigging, were dyed red. To add to this striking image, the Vikings' shields were hung from the side of the boat, which provided protection as well as adornment.

But these ships were more than beautiful; they were powerful. They had a shallow draft, which means they did not need deep water to sail. They were propelled both by a sail and a bank of about 50 oars, which made them highly maneuverable. Longships were identically pointed at both ends, which means they did not have a designated front or back—a lifesaver in dangerous situations when they needed to change directions quickly. They could navigate almost anywhere, which was helpful as they were used for trade and commerce as well as for raiding.

Vikings were often buried with their ships, which means that a large number of the ships have survived and been unearthed. Careful study of these vessels and burial sites has explained a lot about Viking ships as well as Viking daily life. Many carefully preserved Viking longships are on display in museums around the world.

he never quite forgave Lagertha for trying to fend him off with her animals. Eventually, he fell in love with a princess named Thora and obtained her father's permission to wed her. Ragnar divorced Lagertha, leaving her to raise their three children alone. She eventually remarried, though her new husband's name is lost to history.

Ragnar had a lot of enemies, and eventually it became clear to him that he could no longer fight them all off by himself. He sent out a distress call to friendly nations, including Norway, hoping that someone would come to his aid to help him protect his throne. Lagertha, who according to Saxo still loved Ragnar (despite his earlier comment that she "spurned his mission in her heart, but feigned compliance"), sailed off to Denmark to help her ex-husband. She brought with her a mighty army, which put Ragnar's ragtag one to shame. With her "matchless spirit," she rallied the troops and led a sneak attack to the enemy's rear, which turned the tide of the war. Once again, Lagertha's troops became the unlikely victors in battle. Clearly she had a talent for winning wars, and Ragnar benefited from that talent not just once, but twice.

Apparently, the massive battle in Denmark had not slaked Lagertha's desire for battle, but instead had stoked it. When she returned to Norway, she had a joyful reunion with her new husband . . . and then murdered him later that night with a spearhead she had concealed in her dress. She proceeded to claim his title and his throne for herself and ruled in his place. Saxo concludes that "this most presumptuous dame thought it pleasanter to rule without her husband than to share the throne with him."

Lagertha's story is unique because her desire for payback was not limited to those who had done her wrong. When King Frey first threw her in a brothel, he lit a fuse on Lagertha's rage, and whomever was around when it blew would suffer her wrath. Her desire to enact revenge on the man who put her in the brothel, and then on any man who tried to rule over her afterward, led her to become a powerful pirate who changed the outcome of several battles almost singlehandedly.

As incredible as she was, Lagertha is just one of the many Viking women featured in the pages of the *Gesta Danorum*. Viking history is littered with courageous female fighters who amazed everyone they encountered with their beauty and strength. Book 3 tells the story of Sela, a "skilled warrior with experience in roving." *Roving* is another word for the land and sea raiding that Vikings and pirates did. Her brother Koll (also called Koller or Kolles) was the king of Norway. He had a deadly rivalry with a pirate named Horwendil (sometimes Orvendil), whom he felt was more popular and had more glory than the king himself. Koll set off on a hunt to find Horwendil and challenge him to a fight to regain his reputation. Koll tracked the pirate to the waters near a deserted island and invited him to meet on shore. After they met, the two men decided that yes, they needed to fight each other; yes, they should fight in single combat because that was the manliest way to do it; and yes, the winner had to bury the loser with full funeral rites because that was the most honorable outcome.

These two men, who might have become powerful allies had they considered talking out their differences instead of rushing into a fight to the death, proceeded to duel. Both men were skilled fighters, but Horwendil's bold fighting tactics were too much for King Koll, and he lost his foot and then his life. Horwendil, as promised, buried Koll with proper pomp and circumstance. Afterward, Saxo adds that Horwendil "pursued and slew Koll's sister Sela."

Why did this fearsome pirate, so concerned with etiquette, feel the need to kill his defeated opponent's sister? How long did this side quest of vengeance take? Did Sela even know, as Horwendil came closer, why she was being hunted? Or was her death a total surprise? More important, did Horwendil honor Sela with the funeral rites he bestowed upon her brother, or was her body tossed aside (or worse)? Saxo did not see fit to share any more of the story with his readers, so these questions remain unanswered.

Another Viking woman whose brother brought about her death was Rusla, featured in Book 8. She is sometimes referred to as Rusila, but Rusila was a different woman altogether, who fought joined forces with her sister Stikla to conquer King Olaf's kingdom. Rusla, like Lagertha, is sometimes linked to a mythical figure. Rusla's story is tied to *Ingean Ruadh* (Gaelic for "Red

Maiden") because of her vicious style of fighting that
tended to spill a lot of red blood. Rusla's brother Tesondus had been the king of Norway but lost the kingdom
to the Danish king, Omund.

Rusla was devastated by the loss of her family's
pride and refused to see her beloved country ruled by
the Danes. She could not understand why her brother
allowed the Danes to take over, so she decided to take
matters into her own hands. She declared war on everyone in her country who pledged allegiance with the
Danes. When King Omund sent soldiers to end her
rebellion, Rusla and her army destroyed them. This
gave her an idea: why fight your own people when you
can fight your oppressors instead? She planned to take
on Denmark by herself, and then rule both Denmark
and Norway on her own.

She invaded Denmark but was beaten back by the
Danish forces. During her retreat, she ran into Tesondus, the cause of the whole situation. She stripped him
of all his men and ships but refused to kill him. That
decision turned out to be fatal. When King Omund sent
his forces to attack Rusla at home, Tesondus was with
them. He captured his sister and killed her. Some versions of this story say that he beat her to death with a
ship's oar. King Omund was grateful to the traitorous
coward Tesondus and gave him a governorship. So, for
attempting to save her country, Rusla was murdered.
For failing to save his country, Tesondus was given a
high-ranking political job.

Book 8 also tells of three female longship captains, although frustratingly few details are provided. Wisna, Webiorg, and Hetha had the bodies of women, but "the souls of men," according to Saxo Grammaticus. Each story has only a few sentences. Wisna was a standard-bearer in battle. In Viking times, the standard-bearer was a person who carried the flag of her nation into the fighting. It was a highly dangerous job that required a massive amount of courage, since the standard-bearer would naturally be a target for the other side. Wisna lost her right hand in combat. Webiorg killed a champion fighter before being killed herself. Hetha was appointed the ruler of Zealand, which is part of modern-day Denmark.

~~~~~~~~~~~~~~~~~~~~~~~~

TEXTILES AS TEXT

Viking sagas were told by Scandinavian men and later recorded by Christian men, so women were often left out of the accounts of Viking history. Or were they? New research by scholar Lena Norrman suggests that Viking women may have recorded history in their own way, by weaving of tapestries. The Överhogdal tapestries, from around the year 1000, tell the story of a dragon slayer, Sigurd, and predate the earliest written record of the legend by nearly 200 years. These tapestries highlight aspects of the story that resonate with typical female listeners, such as love, honor, and passion, instead of the more conventionally masculine aspects of the tale, such as the killing of the dragon and the quest for gold.

With the information contained in these tapestries, historians can now examine the female perspective on events from this era, previously thought to be lost to time. "Silent" women still made their voices heard through their art. What other "silent" women's voices can be discovered through the exploration of nontraditional recording of history?

The Viking Age ended around the 11th century, closing the door on the era of Lagertha, Sela, Rusla, and all the others. Most Vikings found places to settle and assimilated quite well into the cultures of their new homelands, disappearing from history. But the Viking spirit lives on, even to the present day. Stories abound of other women pirates from the Scandinavian region long after the end of the Vikings, such as Christina Anna Skytte, Elise Eskilsdotter, Ingela Gathenhielm, and Johanna Hård. Clearly, the drive to escape ordinary life and become someone greater has persisted long after longships went out of fashion.

Learn More

Druett, Joan. *She Captains: Heroines and Hellions of the Sea*. New York: Simon and Schuster, 2000.

Grammaticus, Saxo. *Gesta Danorum*, trans. Oliver Elton. New York: Norroena Society, 1905.

Stanley, Jo, ed. *Bold in Her Breeches: Women Pirates Across the Ages*. London: Pandora Press, 1995.

Part II
Escape

Alfhild

Many little girls love princesses. And why not? In fairy tales, princesses live perfect lives. But like most things, there is more to being a princess than what the stories tell. Not all princesses are happy; some yearn to be anything other than who they are. Princess Alfhild (also called Awilda) became a pirate because she wanted an escape from her life—an escape that tragically was just beyond her reach.

Alfhild's life was described in several different books. Like Lagertha, the main account of her life comes from the *Gesta Danorum*. Other accounts contain many factual errors and have been discounted, although the stories continue to spread. Finding the truth about Alfhild is difficult, but there are enough similarities among the legends to piece together a basic biography upon which most scholars can agree.

Alfhild was born sometime around 790 CE. Her father, King Siward, was king of the Goths. The Goths were an east Germanic people whose fighting prowess was so strong that at one time they controlled the entire region from the Black Sea to the Baltic Sea. Alfhild's status as a Gothic princess meant that she was very valuable to her kingdom. Her father could use her as a diplomatic bargaining chip to secure an alliance with another tribe or gain other things of value. During this era, women were often viewed as property instead of as people. Their worth came from what their male relatives could trade for them. Alfhild, as a princess, was worth a lot.

In addition to being valuable to her family, Alfhild was said to be very beautiful and modest. To keep men from being stunned by her beauty, she wore a high-collared robe at all times so she could hide her face when men were near. Whose idea this robe was, the story doesn't say. Was it Alfhild's father's plan to surround his daughter with mystery and thus make her a more attractive commodity? Was it her mother's plan to keep Alfhild from gazing lovingly at any of her suitors and possibly falling into temptation? Or did Alfhild decide to wear the robe so she could go about her daily life without lustful men constantly leering at her?

Despite this precaution, men far and wide heard of Alfhild's beauty, and many came to ask for her hand in marriage. Her father was pleased in the quality and quantity of offers for his daughter's hand, but King Siward was not content to sell her to the highest bidder.

VIKING SAGAS

Long before the *Gesta Danorum*, the Viking people first passed down the stories of their ancestors in long poems called sagas. Sagas were performed at feasts and in the halls of royalty. There were several different types of sagas. Some were about kings and queens and battles, whereas others had mythical and fantasy figures as their subjects. The Vikings did not use written language in their everyday life, so these sagas were not committed to writing during the time the Vikings lived and ruled.

A few centuries after Alfhild's time, the Vikings were Christianized and began to tell their stories to people who recorded them in Latin. With so much time between the events in the sagas and their Latin transcriptions, the stories in the sagas likely went through many changes. Therefore, it is impossible to know how accurate the stories are. However, historians have verified that many of the people featured in the sagas did exist, and that the sagas are the best resource available to learn about the Viking people. History must be taken as it is found, not as historians wish it could be found.

He wanted a spectacle, something to get people talking and prolong the contest for Alfhild. He sheltered Alfhild in a high tower and gave her two snakes as bodyguards. To have a chance to marry Alfhild, the king decreed, a potential suitor had to defeat the snakes. If a man attempted the task and failed, he would be killed by the king. His head would be displayed on a pike for all to see, warning other men to think very carefully before trying to win the right to marry the princess.

Many men lost their heads over Alfhild before Prince Alf came along. Alf, son of King Sigar of Denmark, was a brave and handsome young suitor. He was not put off by the snakes or the threat of beheading—he was, after all, a Viking man, used to difficult living conditions and the near-constant threat of death. He knew he would have to come up with something special to get past the snakes, and he did. He covered himself in blood, which upset the snakes and impaired their senses. The crazed snakes were easier to slay: one got a spear to the mouth, the other a red-hot steel rod. With both of them out of the way, Alf was free to claim his princess.

However, the blood-covered prince was not entirely done with his quest. As a final hurdle, the princess herself had to claim Alf. As part of the spectacle of the contest, Alfhild's father, King Siward, made her acceptance a condition of the betrothal. Siward probably thought the young maiden would leap at the chance to marry a brave, intelligent man who had dispatched her scaly babysitters and wanted to spring her from the tower. After all, what kind of girl says no to a handsome prince?

It turned out that Alfhild was that kind of girl. Nobody is sure why she refused Prince Alf. Some say her mother talked her out of marrying him, though why her mother would do such a thing is a fascinating question to consider. Other people say she made the decision herself. No matter why she ultimately decided that a life married to Prince Alf was wrong for her, all versions of the story agree that the offer was refused. After the prince was sent away, Alfhild escaped from her tower, her family, and her entire way of life. She and her handmaiden, Groa, slipped out of the castle and became pirates.

How she could have pulled off such a thing is hard to understand. After all, the stories about her life before her botched betrothal do not mention her having any sailing skills. Life aboard a Viking longship was famously difficult. Could a princess used to luxury in a tower survive on the high seas?

Some versions of the story claim that she happened upon a group of sailors who took one look at her beauty and instantly made her captain. A bevy of trained sailors would help to explain Alfhild's ability to function at sea, but the idea that a group of men dependent on their captain's leadership to make a living (and stay alive) would cast everything aside for a pretty face seems far-fetched. However, people are known to do extraordinary things in extraordinary circumstances. Alfhild could have learned to sail, found some sailors who knew how to sail, or ended up on a ship in a different way. The world will probably never know for sure.

However they did it, Alfhild and Groa became pirates—for a while. How long exactly, the accounts do not say. Prince Alf mounted several expeditions to find her, so it makes sense that Alfhild was gone for at least as long as it took to put together a serious search party a few times in hospitable weather conditions, possibly a year or more. According to the stories, Alfhild performed deeds "beyond the valor of a woman," which makes it seem like she was successful in her pirate raiding. She was, at the very least, able to stay afloat and elude her would-be "rescuers" for a while.

For Alfhild to survive aboard a Viking longship, never mind to do any raiding, required extreme strength and bravery. Viking ships were not meant for beginner sailors. Typically, they were around 100 feet long, with lean wooden hulls. The ships were made with overlapping wooden planks held together by iron nails, which is called clinker-style construction. While they were extremely efficient sailing and fighting ships, they were not designed with creature comforts in mind. The ships did not have living space, so Alfhild and her crew would have had to sleep on shore in leather sleeping bags with their weapons at arm's reach, even in the rain, snow, and powerful hot and cold spells. They ate almost exclusively raw meat, with not a fresh vegetable or fruit in sight. Watch for enemy ships was kept around the clock, which means sleep was always in shifts and disrupted. Viking first aid was not advanced. For example, dogs licked warriors' wounds clean to ward off infection.

This primitive life was not for anyone but the bravest and strongest, and Alfhild succeeded in enduring it.

~~~~~~~~~~~~~~~~~~~~

VIKING MYTHOLOGY

Although Viking warrior culture was packed with "manly" images and heroes, it produced more than its fair share of female warriors. This might be due in part to the fact that Viking mythology is full of female figures who play vital roles in battle. For example, at the roots of the Vikings' tree of life, Yggdrasil, lived the Norns. These female beings, similar to the Fates of Greek mythology, controlled the destinies of all—both humans and gods. Powerful male gods, such as Thor and Odin, were still subject to the whims of the Norns. In their hands the Norns held life, death, and everything in between. Women, not men, ruled the Norse world.

Norse mythology also includes the Valkyries. These attendants of the powerful god Odin moved untouched through the Viking battlefields, choosing from among the wounded those who would live to fight another day and those whose battle had permanently ended. Among the dead, they picked who would go on to glorious Valhalla, the heavenly dining hall where warriors feasted for eternity and stood at the ready to assist Odin during Ragnarök, the Viking version of the end of the world. The Valkyries are portrayed as beautiful and noble, but also sinister. One story depicts them gleefully cackling as they weave the tapestry of fate made of human intestines.

These mythical women, along with the other powerful Old Norse goddesses, exist alongside men and also

perform a vital part of battle rituals. They are not confined to home and hearth, tearfully waiting for their husbands and sons to return to them after the fight is over.
They are in the thick of it, making plans and choosing
warriors for the afterlife. The Norns and the Valkyries
demonstrate that the Old Norse people accepted the
fact that women *did* have a part to play in war.

Even Alfhild, the clever pirate and escape artist,
could not hide forever. The Norns showed their cruelty toward humans when they planned Alfhild's fate.
Eventually, Prince Alf and his men tracked down Alfhild's ship, reportedly walking over a sea of frozen ice to
engage it in battle. The fight was fierce, with both sides
fighting to secure their futures: Alf wanted a wife, and
Alfhild wanted her liberty. Only one of them could win
the future they desired. Borgar, Prince Alf's lieutenant,
was in the middle of a sword fight when he knocked
off his opponent's helmet. It was revealed that his duel-
ing partner was the princess herself—the object of his
search. When Prince Alf realized his beloved was so
near, he knew he must "fight with kisses and not with
arms." He held Alfhild close, kissed her, and ultimately
made her change from her pirating gear into more lady-
like clothes. The battle was over—Alf had clearly won.

Alfhild sailed back home to her father's house. King
Siward was so happy to have her back that he agreed to
Alf's demand that they be married. The fate that Alfhild

worked so hard to escape caught up with her in the end. Her story does not mention how she felt about being captured and forced to marry a man whom she had already said no to once. It also does not mention how she felt about returning to a life of wifely domesticity on land after such daring exploits at sea. Was she resigned to her fate, or did she harbor some hope that someone might intervene and set her free? Was she sad, or was she furious? Could she possibly have been happy?

The world knows about Alfhild from the Christian authors who wrote down the story the Norse people told them, many centuries after the events in the story took place. The transcribing authors may have changed parts of the story, or made up new parts, to make it serve their purposes. The church during this era was incredibly powerful and exercised control over all aspects of life. It was very important to the church that family order be maintained. Women were supposed to take care of things inside the home, such as children and cooking and cleaning. If women ran off and became pirates, who would wash the dishes and make sure that children were educated to become faithful churchgoers? Alfhild's very existence was a threat to the church's message. So, it is possible that her story's fairy-tale ending of riding off into the sunset with the prince is just that—a fairy tale. Maybe Alfhild slaughtered Alf and put his head on a pike. Who knows?

No matter what happened to Alfhild, she is definitely part of history. Her story has been a beloved part of folklore since at least the 12th century, which means it has survived for over 900 years. Thanks to stories like hers, female Vikings have always been popular. In 2017, a Viking grave site long thought to belong to a male warrior was determined through DNA testing to be a female warrior's, which set the Internet into a frenzy. In 2011, an academic study was reported to prove that half of Viking warriors were women. Although that is not exactly what the study said, the fact that people were so enthusiastic about that result shows how excited people are to believe that there were women Viking warriors.

Alfhild did not live the life of a typical princess. Her ride into the sunset with the handsome prince was not entirely joyful. The one thing she sought for herself—freedom—she did not get. Still, she was courageous and brave, and (for as long as she could) she rejected a life chosen for her and instead made a whole new life for herself. Her escape may have been temporary, but it has permanently enshrined her story in history and in the hearts of women everywhere.

Learn More

Druett, Joan. *She Captains: Heroines and Hellions of the Sea*. New York: Simon and Schuster, 2000.

Grammaticus, Saxo. *Gesta Danorum*, trans. Oliver Elton. New York: Norroena Society, 1905.

Moen, Marianne. *The Gendered Landscape: A Discussion on Gender, Status and Power in the Norwegian Viking Age Landscape*. Oxford, UK: Archaeopteris, 2011.

Margaret Jordan

A popular pirate adage proclaims that "dead men tell no tales," but living pirates (especially pirate women) don't tell very many tales either. History has been left with few first-person accounts of pirate women. There are no diaries and few letters. The primary source documents that exist are from people nearby, such as victims and others who dealt with the pirates. These reporters can provide facts but cannot tell us what these women were feeling, why they became pirates, and which dreams they held closest in their hearts.

In this sparse field of women who spoke for themselves on the record, Margaret Jordan is a shining example of why women *should* tell their stories. She was a pirate who testified at court in her own defense. Her words tell us her version of the story, pure and unedited by any other person. Her account is at odds with the other accounts of the incident, but her words are more powerful than the other accounts. Her words were strong enough to save her life and finally grant her the escape she had been seeking for so long.

Margaret Croke was born in Ireland during the last half of the 18th century. Virtually nothing is known about her childhood or upbringing. She entered history as a young woman at her marriage to Edward Jordan in 1798. He was a handsome man with dark hair and eyes and very white teeth. His attractive looks masked his troubled spirit, which would cause his bride a world of distress in the years to come. Edward came into the marriage with a long criminal history. His reputation as a rebel and a troublemaker was large, and there were rumors he had narrowly escaped being executed by scrambling over a prison wall.

To be sure, Edward was Catholic during a time when it was not easy to be Catholic in Ireland. Ireland would not be fully independent and escape British control until 1919, over a century after Edward's time. During his lifetime, the country was controlled by Anglicans, who were Irish Protestants loyal to the British crown. The government discriminated freely against Edward and all Catholics by not allowing them to vote, apply for state jobs, or run for Parliament, among other things. Edward worked as a landlord's deputy, where he was tasked with evicting families from their farms at the whims of an unseen landowner. Naturally, this was bad news for the people being evicted, and Edward unfairly bore the brunt of their anger. His life situation instilled in him a hatred of the British, and he joined the Society of United Irishmen to fight them. Just before his marriage, he served in the Battle of Wexford, which was a significant defeat for the British.

History does not say whether Margaret didn't know about her husband's violent past or just wasn't bothered by it. Their marriage was a love match, and in the beginning they were happy. The newlyweds lived with Margaret's father for a year. They survived a legal battle for Edward, who was arrested for not having his papers in order. They moved out of her father's house and tried life in another part of Ireland for four years but found no success there either. The Jordan family, which now included several daughters, decided that the New World could offer them a better life. They immigrated to the United States and, according to Margaret, that was the end of their happy marriage.

~~~~~~~~~~~~~~~~~~~~~~~

IRISH IMMIGRATION TO NORTH AMERICA IN THE EARLY 19TH CENTURY

Margaret's family left the green hills of Ireland to chase the dream of a new start in America. They were far from alone in this dream. Around 50 years after the Jordans arrived on US soil, there were more Irish-born people in New York City than there were in Dublin. Irish people were just under half of the American immigrant population in 1850. Many came for economic opportunities, like the Jordan family did. Countless others were driven to leave home by a massive famine that starved hundreds of thousands. When they arrived in the United States, they had little except hope for a new life.

Many of those hopes were not realized. Protestant Americans were afraid of the mainly Catholic Irish immigrants, worried that the pope would use them to somehow gain control of America. Anti-Irish sentiment was high during the 19th century, and many stores and boarding houses displayed signs reading No Irish need apply. Forgetting that they themselves were new to the country a few generations earlier, the Americans subjected the Irish immigrants to all kinds of prejudice and violence.

This prejudice lingered on through the US Civil War. It would take Irish Catholic John F. Kennedy's election as president of the United States to make the Irish feel they were truly part of American society. The long struggle the Irish underwent for equality is a reminder that people often fear newcomers for no reason, a sad trend that continues today.

What happened to the Jordan family in the United States isn't entirely clear, but they did not stay in the country long. The family moved farther north to Canada. They lived in several different regions of the country, working various odd jobs, but they never found the prosperity they sought. They ended up in Percé, on the

Gaspé Peninsula in Quebec. It was, at the time, a small seasonal fishing village known for its attractive geography. The Jordan family briefly attempted farming there before eventually deciding to give the local trade a try. Edward Jordan joined the fishing business, hoping that at last he had found a job and a town that would stick.

To become a fisherman, Edward needed a boat. He couldn't afford one himself, but he figured he could find someone who would invest in one (and him) for a share of the profits. Edward made a contract with a wealthy family, the Tremaines, who were citizens of Halifax, some 500 miles away. Their bargain was simple: if the Tremaines paid the money up front to purchase the ship, Edward would repair it so it could be used as a commercial fishing ship and then pay them back for his portion of the ship's price once the fish started rolling in.

Edward went back to Gaspé with everything he would need to fulfill his end of the bargain. He completed the repairs on the purchased ship, now named the *Three Sisters*. When everything was shipshape, Edward set sail on the *Three Sisters* to Halifax. All parties agreed on these events up to this point. But after Edward arrived in Halifax, their stories started to change.

According to the Tremaines, Edward returned to Halifax without the money he owed them. He told them that he had some dried fish back home in Percé that, when sold, would cover the money he owed. The family apparently did not believe this excuse and became anxious about letting Edward sail off in the ship without some security that he would come back. They put their own captain, John Stairs, on the *Three Sisters* and sent the pair of men back to Percé to come up with the money. Captain Stairs would become a vital piece of the puzzle at the Jordan criminal trial.

When Edward returned home, Margaret was angry. Not only was he again looking for money, but he had also come back from Halifax empty-handed despite promising to bring her food and clothes for their children. The Jordan girls were starving and dressed in rags, and Edward had made things worse instead of better. Also, he refused to admit he was in the wrong. He felt that he had been cheated, because in his mind he was the true owner of the *Three Sisters*. He had done the work on it. He was certain that he was right, and he was not interested in making amends with the Tremaines. To make matters even worse, when it turned out the promised dried fish would cover only a fraction of what was owed, Captain Stairs repossessed the *Three Sisters* on behalf of the Tremaine family. Now the Jordans were truly out of luck: shipless, penniless, and in massive debt.

The Jordan family's situation seemed bleak, but the worst was still to come. On September 10, 1809, Captain Stairs, three of his men, and the entire Jordan family boarded the *Three Sisters*, headed toward Halifax. Why all of the Jordans joined this voyage is unclear. Stairs claimed he was taking them to Halifax as a favor, so that Edward could clear up some of his debt in person and perhaps appeal to the Tremaines' sense of charity when

Edward and Margaret presented their starving children as evidence of their poverty. Edward believed the opposite: he thought he and his family were going to be thrown in debtors' prison. No stranger to jail, Edward was in no hurry to return, particularly with his family in tow. Debtors during this time could be locked up indefinitely or even transported to a penal colony thousands of miles from home, and the Jordans felt that they had struggled through too much for too long for their story to end with them rotting in jail. Out of options, they hatched a desperate plan to keep their children free.

According to Stairs, on the afternoon of September 13, the Jordans began their attack. Edward and Margaret crept through the ship, stealthily wounding or killing the crew one by one. Edward carried a gun in one hand and an axe in the other, while Margaret wielded a boat hook. She bashed Stairs over the head a few times before he escaped, jumping overboard into the freezing sea. He used a hatch he pried off the ship as a life raft.

With Stairs in the sea and three dead crew members on board, the Jordans had officially captured the ship and turned pirate. Their original plan was to head for Ireland and put as much distance between themselves and Canada as they could. The fatal flaw in their plan was that the 2,500-mile journey could not be made with just the two adults on board; they needed a crew. Since they had just killed their only crewmembers, the *Three Sisters* was forced to dock in Newfoundland to recruit some new ones. Their voyage was delayed numerous times. Although they were in possession of a stolen ship and had just murdered three men, the Jordans seemed almost hesitant to leave Canada. This delay of departure would prove fatal—for one of the Jordans.

John Stairs, the hapless captain who leapt into the sea toward certain death in the icy waters, miraculously survived. He was picked up just three hours after his jump. The lucky captain sailed with his rescuers all the way to the United States, where he reported the ordeal he'd suffered to the British consul. (Canada was still under British control at this time.)

Word traveled through Canada that the Jordans had stolen the *Three Sisters* and killed the crew. On October 20, 1809, the governor of Nova Scotia, Sir George Prevost, made out a warrant for the arrests of Margaret and Edward Jordan. The government offered a £100 reward for their capture, and the Tremaine family matched that reward (around $16,500 total in 2019 American dollars).

Such a large reward meant that everyone was on the lookout for the Jordans. It was no surprise that they were apprehended quickly and put on trial for theft and murder. Governor Prevost was determined to make an example of the Jordan family. He wanted to use their trial to prove that the king's law extended all the way across the ocean to Canada. After the trial, there would be no question of who was in charge in the country.

Prevost convened a special court just for the trial, spending large sums of money to ensure that the trial was picture-perfect. Fourteen men sat on the judges'

CANADIAN WOMEN ON JURIES

Margaret Jordan went on trial for murder in Canada. Canadian law today provides that she would be tried for such a serious offense by a jury, but it wasn't until very recently that women could serve on Canadian juries. In 1952, Manitoba was the first province of Canada that allowed women to serve on juries. Quebec did not allow women to serve until 1971.

In the United States, the accused is allowed to challenge the jury if it doesn't appear to be a true jury of peers (for example, made up solely of white women for a black man's trial, or made up entirely of rural citizens for a crime that took place in the inner city). In Canada, however, the accused is allowed to challenge the jury only if the composition of jury members happened through fraud or other misconduct. This does not happen often, and the challenge is usually not successful. Margaret Jordan would have had to wait 159 years to be tried in Nova Scotia by a jury that included people of her own gender.

bench. The trial was built to impress, and it did, attracting lots of media attention.

At trial, John Stairs presented his version of events. Margaret had a different version, and she presented it to the court as well. She claimed that her husband, a jealous man, hated Stairs because he had previously given the Jordan children some new clothing. On the day of the attack, Edward caught Margaret and John Stairs alone in her cabin—just talking, not engaging in romantic behavior—and flew into a murderous rage. Margaret was so distraught about her husband's anger that she lost her senses and was no longer aware of her actions after that point. She testified on the witness stand that "to the best of my knowledge I did not [beat Stairs with the boat hook]," but she couldn't say for sure due to her emotional state. She told the judge that she was afraid for her children's safety and could have acted out of instinct to protect them. Margaret went on to give an emotional speech detailing the long history of abuse she suffered at Edward's hands. The new crewmembers hired in Nova Scotia agreed with Margaret's testimony, telling of a woman trapped aboard a ship with her murderous husband. Margaret was constantly afraid for her life and the lives of her children.

This moving story affected everyone in court. Not even Stairs's testimony that Margaret had bashed him with a boat hook could overcome her sad, very sympathetic tale of abuse—a mother willing to go to any lengths to protect her children. As a result of her testimony, Edward was found guilty and hanged. Margaret was acquitted. While several accounts claimed that both of the Jordans were hanged, the court report clearly states that Margaret Jordan was found not guilty and released. Some stories even claim that a collection of money was taken up by the friendly Canadians to help resettle the widow and her children in Ireland.

Margaret Jordan is one of only a handful of women who were tried for piracy and acquitted. She walked away from the gallows, free from her abusive husband, and was able to start her life over again. The ability to tell her own story saved her life. Her words, whether they were ultimately true or not, held great weight. For the first time since she married Edward, her destiny was wholly under her control, and she seized the opportunity to rescue herself from death and her children from a life of poverty. Margaret's quest to escape her dire circumstances makes her an excellent pirate, whether or not she raised a hand against Captain Stairs.

Learn More

Druett, Joan. *She Captains: Heroines and Hellions of the Sea*. New York: Simon and Schuster, 2000.

Greenwood, F. Murray. *Uncertain Justice: Canadian Women and Capital Punishment, 1754–1953*. Toronto: Dundurn, 2000.

Charlotte Badger

What is treasure? A hundred different people might give a hundred different answers. Treasure, like piracy, has evolved over time. For example, in ancient times, treasure might have been something vital for life, such as grains, cloth, or vegetables. During a particularly shameful period in American history, human slaves were regarded as treasure. There is also the more conventional idea of treasure: gold, silver, and glittering jewels. Can treasure even have a definition when it can take so many forms? Treasure is anything so valuable that owning it seems almost impossible, yet it is still worth great effort to possess.

For Charlotte Badger, the impossible treasure that she risked her life for was her escape from captivity—her freedom. She did not become a pirate to steal treasure; she became a pirate because she *was* treasure. Her desire for escape created one of the wildest female pirate stories of all time. Her journey spans several continents, her life contains several amazing twists and turns, and her fate remains a tantalizing mystery. Charlotte Badger's story is so incredible that she is famous for more than one reason. Besides being a female pirate, she was also the first white female settler of New Zealand.

Charlotte Badger was born in 1778 in Worcestershire, England. Worcestershire is a rural county in the West Midlands, rumored to be the inspiration for the Shire in J. R. R. Tolkien's *The Lord of the Rings* saga. Her childhood among the green hills did not satisfy her hunger for something more in life. In 1796, 18-year-old Charlotte was convicted of a petty crime, either housebreaking or pickpocketing, depending on the account. Legend has it that she stole a silk handkerchief and a few guineas (British coins used until 1816 that equaled a little over one pound). For this offense, Charlotte was sentenced to transportation for life to a penal colony in New South Wales, present-day Australia.

Although this seems like a harsh penalty, Charlotte was actually lucky. Until 1808, pickpockets were eligible for the death penalty under English law. In her darkest moments, Charlotte could have imagined that death would be better than being shipped halfway across the world, never to see her family or friends again, destined to a life of hard labor.

Charlotte, along with Catherine Hagerty, whom she met during the journey, endured the awful six-month sailing voyage from England to Australia. They traveled on the *Earl Cornwallis*, where conditions were unbelievably bad. Convicts were chained up below deck for the entirety of the trip, never once seeing the sun for six months. Many died on the trip.

Charlotte and Catherine survived, however, and arrived at Port Jackson, Sydney, in 1801. They were assigned to the Parramatta Female Factory, a women's prison. There Charlotte gave birth to a daughter in 1806, father unknown. It is likely that her child was fathered by a jailer or guard, against Charlotte's will. Charlotte's daughter remained with her mother at the factory, as all children did until the age of four. After that, the children of convicts were sent to Orphan and Infant Schools. After the children and their mothers were separated, they usually never saw each other again.

PARRAMATTA FEMALE FACTORY

The Parramatta Female Factory was a large complex that housed a dorm/prison, a factory, and a medical facility for transported women convicts. Approximately 8,300 women spent time in the factory before it was shut down. The factory was modeled after the English workhouses to which poor and criminal women were sent to work off their debts, and it shared the same unsafe living conditions and harsh treatment that made the English workhouses infamous.

Women were divided up into three classes, which determined what kind of work they could do and where they lived. First-class women were eligible for assignment outside the prison and received the best food and jobs, such as weaving and hat making. Second-class women were either on probation or under medical care. Third-class women were serving hard time and only got the worst jobs, such as rock breaking. According to an account from a judge at the time, these female prisoners, whom he called "Amazons," were much worse than the male transports in terms of behavior. The Amazons showed no fear of the armed guards who were sent to squash their rebellions.

Most of the rebellions were caused by unrest resulting from overcrowding in the prison, which was notoriously bad. Being crammed into the jail with no personal space or privacy put many women on edge and made them irritable. Conditions were so bad that sometimes women had to sleep in the factory workrooms among bales of wool because no beds were available. These overworked and underpaid women could leave the prison in four ways: a ticket of leave at the end of the sentence, a transfer to another assignment, death, or marriage.

In an odd twist, the prison ran a sort of matchmaking service to assist the bachelors in the area. Many women married their way out of Parramatta. It is estimated that 1 in 10 Australians today are descendants of these transported convict women.

Somehow, by the end of 1806, Charlotte and her friend Catherine had their sentences commuted. The two women may have demonstrated exceptional behavior or, more likely, caught the eye of someone important at the prison. Perhaps the father of Charlotte's child wanted his daughter to grow up in a nicer place than the factory.

Whatever the reason, these two women were again selected for a sea voyage. They were supposed to travel to Hobart Town, part of present-day Tasmania, to become domestic servants. For this trip, they would be traveling on the *Venus*, a 45-ton brig. The people aboard this historic voyage of the *Venus* were Charlotte, Catherine, Charlotte's daughter, two male convicts, a guard, and the crew. It was a large ship, with two tall masts and square-rigged sails. The captives were housed below deck, just like they were on the *Earl Cornwallis* when Charlotte and Catherine came to Australia. The women might have been given a separate space away from the male convicts, but this was not common practice and far from guaranteed. So, even though they were leaving the prison, the women would not have been happy about this voyage. It was going to be another long and painful journey, with a difficult, unpleasant life waiting for them at the end of it . . . if they survived.

No two accounts agree on what happened after the women boarded the *Venus*. According to some versions, Captain Samuel Chase was an extremely cruel man who regularly beat the women for his amusement. Other stories say the women were generally friendly with the

TRANSPORTATION TO AUSTRALIA

Charlotte Badger was just one of many people transported to Australia. This punishment was an odd solution to a difficult problem plaguing the British justice system. In the late 1700s, social reformers exposed the appalling conditions in England's overcrowded jails and turned popular opinion against cramming more people into the prisons. The other option at the time—execution—did not seem attractive (or even possible) for every criminal convicted by the courts.

So, England had a large body of prisoners, no space to lock them up, and no appetite to kill them all. What could lawmakers do? Since the Revolutionary War, criminals could no longer be sent to America to be disposed of. Where could these criminals be housed?

The answer the justice system came up with was to ship the convicts to the colonies England established in Australia, where they would become essentially slave laborers. From 1788 to 1868, approximately 160,000 convicts were transported. Convicts weren't the only ones who were transported, however. From the 1920s to the 1970s, British children, either orphans or wards of the state, were transported to Australia as well, often facing the same dismal working camps that the prisoners faced a century before.

crew and regularly got into mischief such as breaking into the whiskey stores. Yet another account states that Catherine and Charlotte developed romantic relationships onboard, Catherine with the first mate and Charlotte with a male convict.

The truth of what happened on board is probably a mix of all the stories but will likely never be known for sure. Whatever went on during Charlotte's time on the *Venus*, by June 1806 she had experienced quite enough. She and Catherine decided to mutiny, a crime that was punishable by death. She would have known the risk when she planned to overthrow the ship's captain, so she either believed she had a chance to succeed or no longer cared if she lived or died. Such a brash move demonstrates how miserable life was for the convicts and how even a small sliver of hope for freedom was enough to make them take desperate actions.

On June 16, Captain Chase docked the *Venus* at Port Dalrymple, a town on the mouth of the Tamar River in present-day Tasmania. What happened next is, again, under dispute. Either he conducted some business in town and returned to the ship to find it—to his horror—sailing away without him, or he was onboard when the mutiny happened and was flogged by Catherine. Captain Chase said that the mutiny was started by Benjamin Kelly, the first mate. What *is* certain is the outcome: on June 17, 10 people sailed away from Port Dalrymple on the *Venus*, and Captain Chase was not one of them.

Stealing the ship and making off with the cargo (much of which was the convicts themselves, who were valuable because they had already been paid for by their new employers) turned Charlotte and the rest of the mutineers into pirates, although unconventional ones. Of all the things pirates have stolen over the millennia, very few have stolen themselves.

The newly minted pirates had pulled off a daring escape and were now free. But what next? The men on the ship came together and decided that, for the rest of their journey, women and children were not needed. Whatever further piratical goings-on they had planned, they did not want Charlotte, Catherine, and Charlotte's daughter to be a part of them. How the women felt about this decision is unknown. Perhaps they were enraged that after participating in the mutiny, they were going to be denied a chance to be a part of the pirate crew. Perhaps they were thrilled to be free of the boisterous crew. Or perhaps they were simply relieved that their ordeal at sea was finally coming to an end.

The pirates sailed across the Tasman Sea to Rangihoua Bay, in the Bay of the Islands, New Zealand. The two adult women and one child were left on shore. The men, not entirely without a conscience, decided not to abandon them at the mercy of the elements or any unfriendly native people. The men quickly built them a basic shelter before sailing off into the sunset with the *Venus*. How the women made their way in this new environment, so totally foreign to anything either woman had known before, is a mystery. In 1807, Catherine died, leaving Charlotte and her daughter alone.

What happened next to Charlotte is the biggest mystery of all. Many different stories account for the end of her days, with very few agreeing on how Charlotte Badger died. Most likely, she died in New Zealand. Either natural causes took her, she died by some misadventure of island life such as a snake bite or drowning, or she was killed by the native Māori. During the era when Charlotte arrived in New Zealand, relationships between the Māori and Europeans became very tense. Just a few years after her arrival, the Boyd Massacre occurred, in which 66 European settlers were killed as payback for the unjust whipping of a Māori chieftain's son. In all probability, Charlotte and her daughter most likely died at Rangihoua Bay, free women at last after such a long and painful journey.

However, there are definitely other possibilities regarding Charlotte's fate. In 1826, an American ship, the *Lafayette*, landed in Sydney, Australia. The crew told a tale that the native people shared with them while they were docked in Tonga, an island nation nearby. Some 10 years earlier, an "enormously fat woman" and a young girl had come through Tonga. The woman spoke fluent Māori and told the amazed Tongans about her adventures around the world. She eventually left Tonga aboard an American whaler and sailed off to America with her daughter.

Could that woman have been Charlotte? It seems more than possible. How would the Tongans, so far away, have heard of Charlotte and told her story to the Americans unless she had really been there? The mystery remains of how she and her daughter got from New

Zealand to Tonga in the first place, but for a woman who traveled so far and survived so much, it is not so hard to believe that she made this journey happen.

Such a happy fate—sailing off to America, land of the free, to start a new life—seems like the perfect ending for a woman who desired escape so much that she stole herself to get it. No matter where she ended up, she was a courageous woman who let her dreams of freedom take her to places other white people had, quite literally, never been before.

THE MĀORI PEOPLE

Charlotte Badger may have had encounters with the native population of New Zealand. The Māori have called the islands their home since approximately 1250 BCE. In the hundreds of years that they lived outside the reach of Western visitors, they developed their own strong culture and traditions.

The Māori were originally hunters and farmers. They became warriors and lived a life steeped in warrior culture. Captain James Cook, the famous European explorer, arrived in New Zealand in 1769. His visit there sparked European interest in trading with and perhaps colonizing New Zealand, ending the Māori's self-contained existence.

Māori/European contact was often amicable, at least for the first hundred years or so. There were isolated incidents of murder and cannibalism, but for the most part the Europeans and the Māori were able to trade peacefully. However, the Māori's sovereignty was taken bit by bit: by disease, by conflict, and by Western land annexation. The Māori language was discouraged, and children were beaten for speaking it in schools.

In 1840, the Treaty of Waitangi was signed to protect the rights of the Māori, but in reality it was used to justify the continued taking of Māori land. The once-proud Māori culture began to wither and die as the population declined due to European suppression. It wasn't until the 1960s that the Māoris' protests for fair treatment by the government were finally heard.

Major efforts are currently underway to revitalize the Māori language and culture in New Zealand. Today, tourists can visit indigenous *marae* (meeting grounds), where they can experience the music, dance, art, and language of the Māori. Even the Māori *tā moko* (biographical tattoos) have had a moment in the spotlight—they were featured in the hit 2016 Disney film *Moana*.

Learn More

Byrne, J. C. *Twelve Years' Wanderings in the British Colonies, from 1835 to 1847.* Vol. 2. London: Richard Bentley, 1848.

Druett, Joan. *She Captains: Heroines and Hellions of the Sea.* New York: Simon and Schuster, 2000.

Rees, Sian. *The Floating Brothel: The Extraordinary True Story of an Eighteenth-Century Ship and Its Cargo of Female Convicts.* New York: Hachette, 2002.

Mary Read

Despite the fact that pirates have been roaming the seas since the beginning of recorded time, most popular images of piracy come from a small slice of time—about 10 years. Between 1712 and 1722, the Golden Age of Piracy in the Caribbean, an unprecedented number of pirates converged in a small area for a short period. Blackbeard, Calico Jack Rackham, Charles Vane, and most other famous pirates emerged from this Golden Age.

As with every age of piracy, there were women pirates during this time. Mary Read, one half of the dynamic duo of Mary Read and Anne Bonny, was notable for excelling in not one but two male-dominated careers: piracy and war. Although her resume is impressive, Mary Read's life was filled with deception and sadness. Her entire career, and basically her entire life, was an attempt to escape the destiny that her mother and society planned out for her.

Mary Read pirated in the heyday of the Golden Age of Piracy. But what was the Golden Age, anyway? What caused it to happen? Several factors, both political and geographical, influenced the beginning of the real pirates of the Caribbean. For starters, the Caribbean was a perfect location. Before the days of motorboats, sailing ships were at the mercy of the currents and tides to get from place to place. The Caribbean was a place where many currents met, which made it easily accessible whether a ship was coming from Africa or Europe. The "triangle trade route" (of slaves from Africa; sugar, tobacco, and rum from the Caribbean and colonies; and textiles from Europe) was immensely profitable and popular during this time. Spain had established colonies in South America and regularly sent Inca, Aztec, and other native civilizations' gold back home to Europe on treasure ships and fleets. In short, a lot of goods and money were traveling in and out of the Caribbean on a regular basis. Where there are goods and money (things to steal), pirates will inevitably follow, and they showed up in force.

In addition to established pirates, many unemployed navy men migrated south and put their sailing skills to good use as new pirates. The transition from the navy to piracy was not as odd as it might seem. The navy was, directly and indirectly, one of the primary causes of the rise of piracy in the Caribbean during the Golden Age. Navy sailors were fired during peacetime, and many of these unemployed sailors chose to find a new job as a pirate because so many of the skills needed (such as sailing and navigation) were the same. Also, the navy often treated members of its lowest ranks inhumanely. Common sailors were frequently beaten, starved, not paid the wage they were promised, and kept away from home and family for extended periods of time. Navy life was so miserable that the freedom and equality that existed aboard pirate ships were doubly sweet to the former navy sailors. The navy did very little to actively suppress piracy in the Caribbean until Governor Woodes Rogers arrived in the Bahamas in 1718. Never before and never again were so many pirates active in one location. It was, and still is, the stuff of legends.

Mary Read is absolutely deserving of her place among the legends of the Golden Age. From her birth, it seems she was destined to become the master of deception that she eventually was. When she was born, somewhere near the end of the 17th century, her mother was in a sticky situation. Years before, her husband had disappeared, leaving her with no means to support herself or her infant son. The money she received from her mother-in-law to take care of the elder woman's grandson was all they had to live on.

Shortly before Mary's birth, her brother (and Mrs. Read's only means of financial support) died. Mrs. Read feared being cut off by her mother-in-law, so she hatched a desperate plan: why not pretend that her living daughter was her dead son? So, from her birth, Mary was dressed as and passed off as a boy. The scheme worked—Mary's mother continued to collect money for her "son." It was as if Mary had never been born.

WHO WAS CHARLES JOHNSON?

Pirate history is full of mystery, so it's no surprise that one of the most famous pirate history books ever written is also surrounded by mystery. *A General History of the Robberies and Murders of the Most Notorious Pyrates*, commonly referred to as "General History of the Pirates," was published in 1724 by the London publisher Charles Rivington and has been in print ever since. Its colorful accounts of the lives and legends of many Golden Age pirates, including Blackbeard, Mary Read, and Anne Bonny, captured the imagination of the reading public and created the modern image of what a pirate should be. Such a popular book, published in many editions and languages around the world, would make the author a fortune . . . if only the author was known.

Captain Charles Johnson, the listed author of the book, is considered to be a pseudonym, since no Captain Charles Johnson is listed in the Royal Navy muster rolls from the correct period. Who was the real author? Over the years, scholars have considered various authors, including Daniel Defoe, author of the famous sea adventure novel *Robinson Crusoe*. The author's knowledge of sailing and the sea suggests that he may have been a sea captain, but nobody knows for sure. The authorship of this critically important book will probably always be up for debate.

Until her grandmother died, Mary lived as a boy. When her grandmother passed away, Mary's mother lost her source of income, so she decided that Mary needed to get a job to support the family instead of just posing as her dead brother. She hired Mary out as a footboy to a French woman. Footboys were servants who ran alongside the carriages of very wealthy women to make sure that the ride went smoothly. Only the wealthiest people could afford such a luxury. Although Mary did well as a footboy, she quit that job and started a new one before her true gender was discovered. Mary decided to give up her old life and go to sea. She set her sights on a lofty goal—the Royal Navy.

The Royal Navy was, for a long time, the most powerful navy in the world. It was instrumental in establishing England as a major world power. At the time of Mary's entry into the navy, around the turn of the 17th century, it was a major force to be reckoned with, with 127 battleships and 49 frigates.

So how did Mary, a woman, join the male-only Royal Navy? What exactly did she do while serving there? The details are lost to history. Johnson only says she "enter'd herself on board a Man of War, where she served some time, then quitted it." She likely worked as either a cabin boy or a powder monkey. A cabin boy ran errands, assisted the cook, and climbed into the rigging when the sails needed trimming, among other tasks. A powder monkey ran gunpowder from the ship's hold to the artillery deck during battle. Both jobs were dangerous and low-paying, and neither would have offered Mary the benefits she would have gotten on land as a footboy.

But Mary did not join the navy for money or comfort. She joined to make her own way in the world, to escape the controlling lies of her mother. The navy offered few opportunities for free will—in reality, life on board was famously harsh and discipline was handed out regularly. But at least Mary had chosen that life for herself, instead of having it chosen for her. She worked in the navy for some length of time, exactly how long is unknown, then left for Flanders (part of present-day Belgium) and joined the English army.

WOMEN IN THE ROYAL NAVY

An anonymous writer in 1762 claimed there were so many women secretly in the Royal Navy that they should have their own all-female battalions. While that might have been an exaggeration (though there's no reason not to believe it), the world will never know exactly how many women filled the ranks of the navy during the 18th century, because the very nature of their participation required them to serve in secret.

Countless women lived, fought, and even died as navy men, and no one will never hear their stories. But some women were outed, either accidentally or purposely after they retired, and their stories are a fascinating tip-of-the-iceberg glimpse into the stories lost forever. Besides Mary Read, two other famous women distinguished themselves in the navy.

Mary Ann Talbot started her navy career at age 14 as "John Taylor." She sailed on several ships doing all sorts of jobs, suffered multiple grievous wounds, and was even a prisoner of war for 18 months. Eventually, she was captured by a press-gang. Press-ganging was an officially sanctioned practice in which men were kidnapped and forced to serve on navy ships to fill empty jobs. Mary was forced to reveal her true gender to a press-gang and was kicked out of the navy as a result. Because she had been wounded during her service, she was unable to find other work and requested a pension from the navy. The navy refused her, claiming that since she was a woman, her service was not eligible for a pension. She fought the decision for years, never obtaining all that she was due. She spent some time in debtors' prison and died in poverty at age 30.

Hannah Snell joined the navy after the death of her daughter. As "James Gray," she uneventfully retired and somehow successfully petitioned for a pension, unlike Mary Ann Talbot. Her story attracted a lot of attention and eventually brought her onstage, where she demonstrated military drills to packed houses. Her fame and success could not spare her a tragic end. She contracted syphilis, at that time untreatable, and died in the famous Bedlam Hospital at the age of 68.

In Flanders, Mary was fighting not on sea, but on land. She found that she liked it and particularly liked one comrade in arms, a Flemish soldier. His name has been lost, but he holds the honor of being Mary Read's first husband. When they were not fighting for their lives, they found time to talk and eventually fell in love. When Mary revealed to her comrade that she was a woman, he was overjoyed and suggested that they become lovers. Mary insisted that she would not enter into a physical relationship unless they were married, and so the pair were wed.

The army, for some reason, was not enraged to find that young "Mark Read" was actually a lady, Mary Read, but instead seemed to be amused at her revelation. The pair was discharged from the army, and Mary's regiment put together a merry wedding for the lovers, complete with a wedding gift: a collection of money so the two could get out of the fighting business and start a new life as tavern keepers. They bought a tavern in Breda (part of present-day Holland) and named it the Three Horse Shoes. The newlyweds ran the successful tavern in wedded bliss until Mary's husband died.

Losing her husband was bad enough, but Mary also lost her business after his death. During the war there were plenty of soldiers and officers to patronize the Three Horse Shoes, but once the fighting was over, people returned home and business dried up. Poor Mary found herself in the same position that her mother had been in years before: without a husband or any means of income.

But where Mary's mother had sold out her own daughter as a way to make money, Mary ruefully cast off her women's clothing and dressed in her fighting uniform. She reenlisted in the army but was unable to support herself because it was peacetime, and well-paying jobs were scarce when there was nobody to fight.

So, Mary left the army once again and headed to a warmer climate—the Caribbean. She sailed on a ship headed to the West Indies, determined to make her fortune somewhere new. What a tumultuous life Mary led! She changed jobs, homes, and even genders so many times to find happiness, safety, and her own place in the world. No matter what misfortune knocked her down, she kept getting back up again and trying something new.

During the 18th century, the Caribbean was not an ideal place to start over. People did not go there unless they had a reason to do so. It was hot, disease-ridden, and full of crime. Only a woman like Mary, someone with nothing left to lose, would risk her life in such a place. Who knows what she would have done or become if her ship had made it to the West Indies?

But fate intervened, and Mary never arrived there. On her way, her ship was taken over by pirates. The passengers were given a choice: join or die. Mary (dressed as Mark again) signed up with the pirates. No doubt the pirates felt lucky to have found such a highly experienced sailor and former navy man in their clutches. Once again, Mary was under someone else's control.

The fact that Mary ended up a pirate is not particularly surprising. What happened to her after she arrived in the Caribbean *is* surprising, even legendary. By chance, Mary Read became part of Jack Rackham's crew. Rackham, known as Calico Jack due to his fondness for flashy clothing made of calico, was a small-time English pirate whose eventual claim to fame was the *two* women who were part of his crew.

Mary, still dressed as Mark, joined up with Rackham and attracted the attention of Anne Bonny, a female pirate and Jack Rackham's lover. Anne quickly became friends with Mark and began spending so much time with "him" that Calico Jack became jealous. Eager to avoid being in the middle of a lover's quarrel, Mary revealed to Anne, then Jack, that she was not a handsome young male sailor but a female one, and so Jack had nothing to worry about. Mary and Anne remained close friends and sailed together on many amazing adventures. Those stories can be found in Anne's chapter in part IV, "Adventure."

When Mary was captured by pirates, she thought her life had hit a dead end, again. Her dream of escaping the control of others had failed her. Little did she know that the biggest adventure of her life—the freest she would ever be—was just about to begin. Her determination to dust herself off and start again after misfortune, no matter how bleak life seemed, paid off in a way she never even knew to hope for. By pursuing escape, Mary Read became a poster girl for a free woman.

Learn More

Cordingly, David. *Seafaring Women: Adventures of Pirate Queens, Female Stowaways, and Sailors' Wives.* Reprint ed. New York: Random House, 2001.

Cordingly, David. *Under the Black Flag: The Romance and Reality of Life Among the Pirates.* New York: Random House, 2006.

Defoe, Daniel. *A General History of the Pyrates.* Mineola, New York: Dover Maritime, 1999. (Previously published as Johnson, Captain Charles. *A General History of the Robberies and Murders of the Most Notorious Pyrates*, London: Charles Rivington, 1724. There are numerous editions of this book.)

Rediker, Marcus. "When Women Pirates Sailed the Seas." *Wilson Quarterly* 17, no. 4 (Autumn 1993): 102.

Part III

GLORY

Artemisia

Artemisia, one of the first female pirates on record, was many things: a queen, a warrior, a sailor, and a pirate. Her story is fairly well known, largely due to her inclusion in Herodotus's *Histories*, a crucial historic record. However, when Artemisia's name is mentioned, the word *pirate* is usually left out. Why is she not more widely known as a pirate? Was she actually a pirate, or has she just been labeled one long after her death? What is the truth and what is fiction? Even in history, that is not always clear. History changes based on who is telling it. After all, whether Artemisia was a Greek hero or a Persian coward depends on whose account is read. Readers have to decide for themselves, not just about Artemisia but about all history.

But is it accurate to call Artemisia a pirate? To be fair, ancient Mediterranean piracy does not resemble the modern conception of piracy. Ancient pirates were not single outlaws who were villains of all nations, solely out for profit. They were more like soldiers, fighting for their own countries on land and sea. However, their methods—such as lying in wait for their prey; sneaking up on larger, heavier ships; using their speed and maneuverability to escape; and adapting their attack methods to their local geography—served as a blueprint for the pirates who came after them. Also, these ancient pirates embodied the spirit of piracy by following their desires to sea and taking others' riches. Artemisia's quest for glory—by any means necessary—is a true piratical tale and an example for all the glory-seeking pirates who came after her.

She was born sometime in the fifth century BCE to a Carian father and a Cretan mother. Her father was the governor of Halicarnassus, a large city-state in the Carian region (part of modern-day Turkey). She grew up by the sea, destined to marry well due to her father's status. Her childhood is a mystery because very little is known about day-to-day life in Halicarnassus. In 500 BCE, she married the king of Halicarnassus. Very few facts have been discovered about their marriage, and even the king's name has been lost to history. He died shortly after their marriage but not before fathering one son. When the king died, the widowed Artemisia ascended to the throne of Caria and ruled by herself in her husband's place.

Artemisia performed all her queenly duties well, including waging war against rival city-states. She not

HERODOTUS'S *HISTORIES*

In 440 BCE, Herodotus wrote what is now considered to be the first modern history book. Before it, historical records were written down, but this work established history as a legitimate study and something worth exploring. It details the politics (both in war and in peacetime), cultures, and geography of the known peoples of Greece, present-day western Asia, and present-day northern Africa.

The book is incredibly impressive but far from perfect. After all, Herodotus was just one man. His biases toward the Greeks and against women are clearly seen in his work. Although he does not record events impartially, as no human can, his careful study of the wars between the Greeks and the Persians, as well as the rise of the Persian Empire, is absolutely worthy of study.

The book is divided into nine smaller books, each named after one of the nine Greek muses. It was composed after Herodotus traveled through much of the ancient world. Herodotus hailed from Halicarnassus, also the birthplace of Artemisia.

only commanded her military forces from her palace but also sailed with them and sometimes took the helm of her own ship. Whom she was fighting with depended on the ever-shifting alliances of the ancient city-states. During Artemisia's heyday, Caria was under Persian control, so technically Artemisia fought under the Persian banner. However, some sources claim that she hated Persia and was secretly sympathetic to the Greeks. Nobody knows her true feelings, but it is known that she destroyed both Greek and Persian enemies at different times. Perhaps the only true allegiance Artemisia felt was to herself.

Ancient Greece was uniquely ripe for plundering by pirates like Artemisia. First, its mountainous geography made overland travel impossible, so in Artemisia's day nearly all travel between cities was done by sea. Lack of good farmland forced city-states to specialize in particular crops and trade for what else they needed. So members of city-states had to travel a lot for trade, and that travel had to be done by sea.

Without motors, ships were able to sail only during favorable winds and at certain times of the year. Because the Mediterranean Sea is littered with small islands and reefs capable of wrecking a large ship, defined narrow "lanes" became the best way to get from place to place. With ships able to travel only in these narrow routes for a very short time in very specific conditions, every pirate knew exactly when and where the large, booty-laden ships would be on the water. Any two-bit pirate could just lie in wait for a big ship to come sailing by and plunder it, knowing that the heavier, slower ship would have no way to escape.

Even the architecture of ancient city-states reflected the constant threat of piracy. "Twin cities" were constructed: one seaside port by the water and one inland center of the arts and politics. The cities were connected by long walls. The idea was that the important religious temples and centers of commerce were protected inland, far from the reach of the pirates, while the walls connecting the two cities ensured that even under siege, the port cities could transport vital goods to the population centers inland.

Coastal Piraeus and inland Athens are a good example of the twin cities construction. Piraeus was the gateway to the "important" city of Athens—it let food and materials in and kept pirates out. Ironically, this plan to curb piracy often backfired because pirates simply looted the port cities, knowing that the city's army was miles inland and would never arrive in time to stop the pirates.

These factors made piracy a fact of life during the late Bronze Age. Everyone knew that it was an inescapable part of seafaring. Homer's ancient epic, *The Odyssey*, contains reference to pirates; specifically that strangers were asked if they were pirates upon their arrival to a new land. All sailors to unfamiliar parts could expect to be asked if they were pirates (there to do the natives ill) or simply sailors who had come to visit, share news, or trade.

There are only scattered stories from Artemisia's early career. One story tells of her sacking of the city of Latmus through a cunning trick. She and her crew threw a festival right outside Latmus's gates, with dancers, music, and everything else usually present at a festival. When the townspeople opened the gates to check it out, Artemisia and her men threw down their tambourines and picked up their swords, catching the people of Latmus by surprise. She may have participated in many other attacks, or perhaps just a few, but it is clear that by the time of the Battle of Salamis, Artemisia had been sailing for Persian king Xerxes for some time.

Xerxes knew that although he had decimated the Greek army, the navy was still a threat to him. Until he defeated the Greeks at sea, he would not be able to take the isthmus of Corinth (and the rest of Greece). Both sides knew that the tide of the war could be turned with a decisive victory on the sea, so each side sought an opportunity that would increase its own chances of attaining one.

Xerxes had every reason to be worried. Persia's capital city, Sula, was far from the sea, and Persia did not even have a navy before the war. How would his ragged band of barely trained sailors measure up against the Greeks, who had been sailing practically since birth? He was content to keep fighting on land for as long as possible until there was a perfect opportunity to meet the Greeks at sea.

Xerxes believed that the time had come in the fall of 480 BCE. The Greek general Themistocles had laid a trap for the Persians. He sent a spy pretending to be an escaped slave to deliver a message for the Persians. The Greeks had anchored off Salamis, a small island a mile off the coast. If the Persians could get there quickly, they

THE GRECO-PERSIAN WARS

Spanning 50 years, this conflict between the Greek city-states and the Persian empire set the stage for the Peloponnesian War. The Persian forces set their sights on adding all of the Greek territory to their already massive empire.

A first invasion by Darius the Great of Persia captured much of Greece, but he was cut off before he made it to Athens and went home in defeat. His son Xerxes invaded Greece a second time in 480 BCE. To do this, he assembled one of the biggest fighting forces of all time. His army won decisive victories across Greece, including at Artemisium and at the famous Battle of Thermopylae, where 300 Spartans heroically held off the Persian army so that the rest of the Greeks could escape.

The win at Thermopylae gave Xerxes access to Athens and much of mainland Greece, and total victory was in sight. It is at this point that Artemisia entered the war, when total Persian domination of Greece was finally in reach. All that remained was the capture of the Isthmus of Corinth, a key piece of land that divided mainland Greece from the Peloponnesian peninsula to the west.

would catch the Greeks by surprise. In reality, the Greeks were ready and waiting, hoping that Xerxes would take the bait and the Greeks could take the Persians by surprise instead.

The Greeks had picked a perfect place for the battle. The bay off the coast of Salamis was a narrow body of water with only two small exit points. Xerxes knew that if the Persians were able to block the exits from the bay, he would have trapped the Greeks and they would have no choice but to wait to be slaughtered. Still, Xerxes was unsure about taking to sea, even in such a seemingly advantageous set of circumstances. He assembled his team of advisors, which included Artemisia, and asked them what they thought he should do.

Every one of them, except Artemisia, told him to go into battle. She advised him not to go, telling him to save his ships. She reminded him that Athens, his original goal, had fallen. If only Xerxes would be patient, their land forces would continue doing their job and all of Greece would be his soon enough. It was too risky, she said, to engage the superior seamen of Greece on the water, especially when they didn't have to do it. Her prudent words were not what the battle-hungry men of Xerxes's council wanted to hear. They wanted to win the war now, rather than later, and waiting seemed like a cowardly thing to do. Xerxes praised her advice but still readied his fleet for battle, dooming his fleet.

The trap worked exactly as planned. The Greek fleet clustered along the shore, mimicking a scared and cowering position. The Persians sailed into the bay in lines three ships deep. As soon as they did, the Greeks made their move. They surged forward, closing the gap between the two navies and basically pinning the Persian fleet along the mainland shoreline. When the front line of Persians attempted to retreat, they ran into their own second and third lines, causing a massive and deadly traffic jam. The Greek sailors sailed around the edges of the Persian mess, picking off ships one by one. What had started out as an easy win for Persia was quickly shaping up into a devastating loss.

Watching the carnage all around her from the deck of her ship, the *Lykos*, Artemisia realized her predictions had come true. The Greeks were going to defeat the Persians, and her own Carian ships were going to be lost. Already, Persian ships were floating in pieces all around her, and her comrades were dead and dying in the water in front and behind her ship, fallen from sinking wrecks or shot down by Greek archers. The cracks of splintering wood echoed ominously while the screams of dying men filled the air.

Artemisia was not going to die in a battle that she had advised against for a cause she did not believe in. It was time for her to make her escape. She had a big problem: her ship was in the middle of the Persian lines, and her allies were blocking her way out. With the Greeks gaining on her every minute, she made a desperate choice. The *Lykos* slammed into a Calyndian ally ship at full speed, totally destroying it. Some say that before Artemisia did, she lowered her Persian flag and raised a Greek one to confuse the Greek fleet and buy herself more time.

Xerxes was watching the battle with some of his advisors from a high hill above the bay. One of them saw Artemisia's well-known ship sink another ship and pointed it out to Xerxes. Both assumed that Artemisia would only sink an enemy, never an ally. Xerxes is reported to have said, "My men have become women and my women have become men." Xerxes never discovered that Artemisia sunk an ally, because nobody on the Calyndian ship lived to tell the tale.

Thanks to Themistocles's trap, the Greeks won the battle of Salamis, as it came to be called. It was one of the most significant military victories in the ancient world because it gave Greece the momentum it needed to go on the offensive against the Persians and kick them out of Greek land.

Despite Artemisia's wise counsel to Xerxes, and her bravery in battle, she mostly disappeared from history after the battle ended. According to some stories, Xerxes sent her to the city of Ephesus to act as a tutor and governess to his illegitimate sons. Another tale claims that she fell in love with an Ephesian man and killed herself when he rejected her. Both stories give Artemisia a conventionally "feminine" ending to her "masculine" war story, and neither is particularly accepted by scholars. It is possible that the authors of these stories were operating under an agenda, such as anti-woman bias or an attempt to make Artemisia's story a cautionary tale.

No matter how her story ended, the beginning and the middle make a serious pirate legend. Her quest for glory for her city-state led her from home to the throne, and from the throne to the battlefield. She ruled Caria herself, even if she had to sink an ally to do it. Her determination to make her own rules would be followed by the pirate women who sailed in the centuries after her.

Learn More

Herodotus. *Histories*, trans. George Rawlinson. Book VIII. New York: Everyman's Library, 1997.

Ormerod, Henry A. *Piracy in the Ancient World*. Liverpool: C. Tinling & Co., Ltd., 1924.

Polyaneus. *Stratagems of War*, trans. Richard Shepherd. Book VIII, ch. 53. 2nd ed. Gale ECCO, 2010.

Teuta

Artemisia is the first known pirate queen, but Queen Teuta, who lived 250 years later, did much more than just follow in her footsteps. Her desire to become a strong leader made her aggressive. She voraciously fought everyone who stood in her way until she ran out of targets. She was so successful that she made an enemy of the mighty Roman Republic, which ultimately led to her downfall. Ironically, her power worked against her in the fight to bring her to heel. Queen Teuta's story is a fascinating examination of pride, leadership, and "masculine" and "feminine" virtues. It is also an example of what can happen when men think women have overstepped traditional boundaries.

Teuta entered history on the throne, as wife of Illyria's King Agron. Illyria was a large city-state along the coast of the Adriatic Sea, made up of parts of present-day

Croatia, Montenegro, Serbia, Albania, Bosnia, and Herzegovina. King Agron was a war-loving king who spent a lot of time expanding his own lands but not worrying about his health. After his forces captured Aetolia in 231 BCE, he threw a banquet to celebrate. He participated in the party so vigorously that he fell ill. A week later, he died, leaving his wife and infant son behind.

Upon the death of the king usually his son would take his place, but since Pinnes was just a child, Teuta stepped up to rule for him as his regent. This was not unheard of in the life of a kingdom, but usually when a woman ruled as regent, she had a small army of male advisors at her side to guide her. Teuta decided she had a pretty good idea of how things worked, and she would be a queen—not a half-queen or a substitute queen, but a true queen ruling on her own. And she would rule Illyria as she—and no one else—saw fit.

~~~~~~~~~~~~~~~~~~~~~~~~~

WOMEN IN CLASSICAL ANTIQUITY

How did Teuta spend her days? There is little information on the day-to-day life of women in Illyria. Undoubtedly, life varied significantly depending on a woman's wealth and social status. For example, a queen would have a far easier life than a peasant woman. But how was an average woman treated during this period? Well, that depends on where she lived.

In Ancient Greece, women's status changed from city-state to city-state. Athens, known for its love of philosophy and culture, had little of either to share with its female citizens. A woman there was not allowed to vote or own anything other than small gifts, which her guardian could get rid of without her permission. Women were passed as property from father to husband. If a woman's husband died before she did, she was either returned to her father's house or placed under the care of her adult sons. At no point was she allowed the freedom to live her life as she chose.

In Sparta, life was a little less severe. In that war-loving society, readiness for battle was above all, and girls as well as boys were athletically trained. Since women had to run things while the men were off at war, they were given greater freedom and allowed to inherit wealth from their families as well as seek divorce.

Most other places in the region fell somewhere in between these two extremes, but in no place was a woman allowed to be above or even equal to a man.

Queen Teuta's first order of business was a bold one. She gave every ship in Illyria's navy permission to attack the ships of other city-states, even ones with whom Illyria was currently at peace. Her husband had enjoyed conquering by land, and now Queen Teuta would expand Illyria's domination to the sea as well. Her act basically turned Illyria's navy into a fleet of pirates. These pirates took to their work with gusto and captured many ships. The treasure they took they brought home, filling Illyria's coffers.

Teuta's newly created pirates flourished under her direction. They exploited the twin cities concept to the fullest extent by capturing ports while the armies were inland, sneaking away before the armies had time to arrive and fight. Teuta did not just command her pirates from the throne, she also sailed with them. Once, she sailed to a city with her crew and walked right up to the city walls holding water jugs. Teuta and her crew pretended (very convincingly) to be lost and dying of thirst. They cried out for pity and some water. When the people of the town opened the gate, Teuta and her pirates swarmed in and attacked the town, using the swords they had hidden in the water jugs.

Teuta was not content just to pillage close to home. She set her sights farther afield on a dazzling target: the wealthy and prosperous Roman Republic. If she could capture enough Roman ships, she could make a foothold in the Roman Republic and maybe eventually annex its territory.

By this time, Teuta had proved to be a savvy and successful pirate, so why should she believe that going after Rome would be any harder than what she'd already done? She attacked a number of Roman merchant ships, terrorizing the crew and stealing the cargo of each ship as she usually did. But there was a hitch in her plan: Rome's pride. Rome did not react the way that the other, smaller city-states did when their ships were attacked, which was to rage at their misfortune but ultimately be unable to stop her. No, Rome would not allow this woman to steal from them.

The republic sent two ambassadors to Queen Teuta to ensure she knew Rome was not going to stand for this behavior. Rome was sending a message: all wayward queens who mess with Rome will quickly be put in their place.

Gaius and Lucius Coruncanius, a pair of brothers, were sent from Rome to Illyria. Their job was to speak with the queen and convince her to issue a ban on attacking Roman ships. Teuta was not impressed, to put it mildly. She replied that the throne of Illyria did not make it a policy to interfere with whom its private citizens chose to attack, no matter who that might be. In short, she rejected Rome's proposal. Lucius, the younger brother, was outraged at the insult to Rome and offered an ultimatum—either issue the ban, or he would make her issue it. Nevertheless, she persisted in rejecting Rome's demands.

There was no help in the Roman rulebook for this situation. Rome issued demands, and Rome's demands were obeyed. Nobody said no to Rome. The negotiators—frustrated, confused, and unsure of what to do next—headed home. When they arrived home, they knew they would not be received happily. However, only one of them made it there. Teuta ordered her men to "kill the one who had used his plainness" in speaking to her, and Lucius was murdered before he returned to his ship.

Rome, understandably, was upset about Lucius's assassination—not upset enough to start a war with the successful queen, but definitely upset.

THE ROMAN REPUBLIC

After the Kingdom of Rome and before the Roman Empire, there was the Roman Republic. Over nearly 500 years, Rome expanded its power from the city of Rome itself to most of the Mediterranean region. During this period, many important events (besides Teuta's battle with Rome) occurred. Rome developed its own navy, which was used to battle pirates like Queen Teuta. The Roman Senate, which had existed in the background during the kingdom period, rose to prominence. The decrees issued by the Senate were supposed to be "advice," but in reality the Senate wielded enormous power thanks to the wealthy and prestigious men who made up its members. Their word might have been sold as advice, but it was followed as law. Also, Rome's first common-law code, called the Law of the Twelve Tables, was composed during this period and posted in the Forum for all to see. The Forum was a flat central area between Rome's seven hills where people could meet, shop, enjoy entertainment such as gladiator fights, and visit temples.

Despite its continued military success, not all was well in the Roman Republic. As Rome expanded more and more, the citizens of the city of Rome suffered. The needs of the people of Rome were secondary to the constant desire of its rulers to expand and conquer. Wars erupted as factions headed by Julius Caesar and Pompey the Great fought and killed each other.

By 27 BCE, Caesar and Pompey were dead and the republic finally fell for good when Octavian, Caesar's nephew, was crowned emperor.

However, Teuta was not done goading them. She decided to reestablish her late husband's land campaign and start annexing territories along the western coast of what is now Greece. She and her royal governor Demetrius marched southward and extended Illyria's borders. They came too close for comfort to the republic's land holdings. Rome could ignore Teuta and her pirates no longer. Teuta had always been annoying to the Romans, but now she had upgraded to alarming and they were forced into action as a result. She was a legitimate threat to the republic's borders, and if Rome wanted to keep all of its land intact, it had to fight her for it.

In 229 BCE, Rome officially entered war with Illyria. Both sea and land campaigns were mounted against Teuta. Ironically, her conquering success would lead to her downfall. Through her previous work in the region, she had left a bad impression in many Greek territories. The Greeks were terrified of her and wanted nothing more than protection from her. So, when Rome marched in, offering to take Teuta down if only they would help out, many city-states gratefully accepted the offer. Places that ordinarily would have put up a fight against Roman domination welcomed the Romans with open arms, since they promised to rid the region of Queen Teuta and her Illyrian pirates. It was a brilliant move on the part of the Romans—using Teuta's own power against her—and it paid off. Rome's land campaign was highly successful, and in no time they had Teuta surrounded.

To make matters worse for Teuta, Demetrius betrayed her to the Romans. He could see that Teuta's time was running out and wanted to make sure that when the fighting was over he was on the winning side. The result of him selling out was that Teuta's sea forces, usually unbeatable, were defeated. The Roman tricksters stole her advantage on land, and her own backstabbing governor took her advantage on the sea. It took a disloyal governor, several countries full of terrified subjects, and the might of Rome itself, but Queen Teuta's unchecked rule of the Adriatic was coming to an end.

Even though she knew her defeat was near, Teuta refused to surrender. She and the remaining troops still loyal to her fled to Rhizon, her capital city, where she had a heavily protected fortress. There they endured a siege for an entire year, surviving starvation as she devised a scheme to get herself out of the mess she was in. Until every last option had been explored, she would not give the Romans the satisfaction of her surrender. Finally, both her supplies and fortifications gave out. She had fought a good fight, but that fight was, at long last, over.

In 228 BCE, Teuta sent a messenger to Rome to negotiate a treaty. The terms she ended up accepting were harsh, which was not surprising given that she clearly had lost the upper hand. She had to pay Rome a fixed sum of money as tribute and give up most of her property, except for a few districts. Worst of all for Teuta, she had to agree not to sail farther than a short distance from her home and could do so only in two unarmed galleys. She would never again sail with a pirate fleet wherever the wind took them. Rome was satisfied with these terms and accepted her surrender.

ANCIENT PIRATE SHIPS

The exact ship used by Teuta and her pirates is unknown, but she probably sailed in either a bireme, a trireme, or a lembus, all of which are types of galley ships.

Galleys were invented by the Phoenicians around 700 BCE. They were long, about 80 to 130 feet, and primarily powered by oars though they were also equipped with sails. They had either two banks of oars (bireme) or three banks of oars (trireme). The oars were on both sides of the ship, with each bank at a different height along the side of the ship so that all sets could row at the same time and not get tangled up with each other. They were built for speed and easy maneuverability, which was a must when trying to get out of tight spots quickly.

The galleys had pointed bows, sometimes covered in metal, which were used for ramming other ships. Before cannons, ramming (sailing at a high speed directly into another ship, causing damage with the weight and force of your ship) was the most effective way to destroy an enemy ship. These galley ships' great power came from human labor—they required anywhere from 100 to 200 rowers, who were often slaves.

Illyrian pirates developed their own special adaptation of the galley ship, called a lembus. Lembi were stripped-down versions of a typical galley, with only one bank of oars and no sails. They were very small and very fast, ideal for pirating.

After Teuta's surrender, she disappeared from history. Nobody knows where she retired, what her career was like after she was no longer queen, or when or how she died. Her story is, at first glance, a sad one. She took on a bigger power than herself and eventually lost. But looking past those surface facts reveals that Teuta's life contained plenty to celebrate. She was a woman who, when given the opportunity to gain some glory for herself and her country, seized it. She did things exactly how she wanted to, no matter what her critics said, and was, for a long time, extremely successful. And when the odds weren't in her favor, when common knowledge dictated she should give in, she kept fighting until the bitter end.

Teuta ultimately teaches us about the glory of refusal: refusal to change her ways to fit in or follow the crowd, and refusal to give up when the going got tough. She proved that saying no can sometimes be as powerful as saying yes.

Learn More

Appian. *Roman History*, trans. Horace White. Vol. 2, Book 10, §7. Cambridge, MA: Harvard University Press, 1912.

Blundell, Sue. *Women in Ancient Greece*. Cambridge, MA: Harvard University Press, 1995.

Polybius. *Histories*, trans. W. R. Paton. Rev. Ed. Vol. 1, Book 2, §4. Cambridge, MA: Harvard University Press, 2010.

Semple, Ellen Churchill. "Pirate Coasts of the Mediterranean Sea." *Geographical Review* 2, no. 2 (August 1916): 134–151.

Part IV
Adventure

Rachel Wall

Not all pirates were driven to the sea by desperate circumstances. Some had perfectly comfortable, average lives on shore, complete with happy homes and families.

Rachel Wall, the first American-born female pirate, was one of those pirates. Although nothing in her story suggests that her life in Pennsylvania was anything but normal, her drive to find something bigger and wilder took her on a journey. This journey, although it ended in heartbreak and punishment, gave Rachel the rebellious life she sought. Her story might be a tale of "be careful what you wish for, because it might come true," but it can also be seen as a tale of a woman who—at least for a time—had a life as big as her dreams.

There are few clues in Rachel's childhood to explain why she ran away and became a pirate. She was born

Rachel Schmidt, one of six children, in 1760. Her parents were hardworking farmers and devout Presbyterians who lived in Carlisle, Pennsylvania Colony. Farmers worked hard labor from before dawn until dusk, and life wasn't easy. However, the Schmidt family did well enough for themselves that their children never went hungry.

The Schmidts' Presbyterian faith put them in the minority of the colony's population. In other colonies, this could have been a source of great tension, but William Penn had worked hard to ensure religious freedom in the Pennsylvania Colony. The Schmidt family could worship without fear, which was very important to them. Religion was the center of their family life. Rachel's parents made the family gather each Sunday to listen to scripture, and they quizzed their children on religious doctrine.

Rachel didn't have a particularly easy life by today's standards, and she might have chafed, as many teenagers do, at her strict religious parents. However, even a boring childhood on a farm would have been a paradise compared to the harsh lives of some of her sister pirates, forced to flee their homes or sold into slavery. So what drove Rachel to piracy?

Rachel got an early start at running away. She snuck out of her home as a child, but she eventually returned on her own. She was welcomed back into her family, like the prodigal son from the Gospel of Luke in the Bible that her parents loved so much. Even that warm reception was not enough to keep her at home, though, and she finally left for good two years later. When Rachel ran away the second time, she left Pennsylvania behind. Did she know when she left that she would never return to her home? History is silent on this detail. Most likely, the teenage Rachel did not have any sadness in her heart as she left her childhood home. She was headed to Philadelphia to start a new life with her secret boyfriend, George Wall.

How did young Rachel meet this man George? There are many stories of how the couple first met. The most common one is that while Rachel was still living at home in Pennsylvania, she attended the funeral of a family friend in a nearby town. During the long funeral, she slipped outside for some fresh air. Some local girls noticed the stranger and started taunting her, and Rachel snapped back at them. Eventually things got physical. George was walking nearby when he saw the dusty pile of thrashing limbs and plucked Rachel out of the fray. They started talking, and romance blossomed.

Perhaps the pair's first meeting was not quite like this, but however they met, they soon fell in love. George convinced Rachel to run away with him and get married. They would start their life together in the big city, far from the drudgery of farm work. The couple went to Philadelphia and New York City before finally ending up in Boston, where Rachel got a job as a maid and George worked as a fisherman.

George Wall, while apparently skilled at breaking up fights between teenage girls, was not a particularly good fisherman. He preferred drinking and having fun with his friends to showing up for his job. Once, he and his buddies threw a party that was so long and so wild, they failed to realize the fishing boat they were supposed to crew had left without them onboard. This unintentional quitting of his job left George in a predicament. No work meant no pay, and no pay meant no food.

With a lot of spare time on his hands, George began to dream up a crazy idea. What if he never had to work for another man again? Could he make a living as his own boss, with his friends for coworkers? Maybe instead of being fishermen, he and his friends could become pirates.

This wasn't as bad of an idea as it sounded. He and his friends had all served as privateers (licensed pirates who worked for a state) during the Revolutionary War. This privateer service had given them a taste of how pirates lived and worked. Because they were fishermen, they had the basic sailing skills necessary for piracy. Further, George had a friend who owned a fishing boat that George could borrow. As long as they brought back some fish each time they took the boat out, they could sail where they pleased without making anyone suspicious. It was a perfect cover story. And so what if piracy was illegal? If they were good enough pirates, they reasoned, they wouldn't get caught.

George shared the idea with Rachel, who agreed to go along with it. The fishing boat was borrowed, and the first voyage of George Wall's band of pirates was officially planned. Most people do not use getting fired as an excuse to turn pirate, but the Walls were not like most people.

The plan was simple: after a storm, make the ship seem like it was in trouble, call for aid, and when it arrived, steal the helping ship and its goods. It was an easy-to-follow plan, but it did require a storm in order to work. Fortunately, there were plenty of storms in New England, where they were sailing. When the weather was right and a storm was brewing, the pirates sailed to the Isles of Shoals and dropped their anchor before the waves got too rough. They rode out the worst of the storm sheltered by the isles, and when the weather started to die down they sailed back toward the coast where they'd come from, right into the path of the shipping lanes. They had purposely rigged the sails incorrectly and flown a distress flag. Now that the trap was laid, all it needed was bait. For this, Rachel would have to do her part. She stood on the deck, weeping and calling out for help. The hope was that the passing ships would be unable to resist a damsel in distress.

ISLES OF SHOALS

The Wall pirate gang chose a particularly significant spot to launch their scheme. The Isles of Shoals, a group of small islands in the Gulf of Maine, have an almost 400-year-old history full of danger, enterprise, and even murder. From the time of their discovery, the islands were used as fishing and trading posts by the Native Americans, the Vikings, and eventually Europeans.

The first officially documented English landing on the Isles of Shoals was in 1623, when Christopher Levett found an abandoned campsite there. After the Levett landing, mainland New Englanders began to set up shop on the islands to take advantage of their strategic location as a stopping point on a sea voyage to Europe, as well as the abundant fishing around the islands.

These settlements prospered until the Revolutionary War, when most islanders left to avoid being attacked by British naval forces. In 1873, the isles became national news when Karen and Anethe Christiensen, sisters-in-law, were brutally murdered on Smuttynose Island by fellow islander Louis Wagner. Approximately 700 ships have been wrecked in the Gulf of Maine.

Eventually, a ship did hear and respond to Rachel's call. The ship's crew allowed Rachel to board their vessel and prepared to take her to safety. These kindly sailors probably fancied themselves heroes, but they had precious little time to enjoy it. On their voyage home, they were overtaken by George and the rest of the crew, who slit all the men's throats and threw their bodies overboard. George, Rachel, and the rest of the pirates took an inventory of what was useful on the ship, stole those useful things, and then sunk the ship. This left no evidence of their robbery and gave them the perfect alibi.

Because ships were often lost during bad storms, nobody would question a schooner gone missing during one.

The first time the Walls pulled this trick, they got around $360 in cash (over $10,000 in 2019 dollars), new fishing gear, and enough fish to sell their story back onshore. Even the fishing gear could be sold. The pirates could claim that it had washed up on the Isles of Shoals, most likely from a shipwreck. All in all, it was a stunningly profitable pirating trip. After her first taste of pirate life, Rachel knew that she would never be satisfied with pulling off a heist like that just once.

Over the years, the pirates honed their routine, murdering 24 people, looting 12 ships, and plundering thousands of dollars' worth of merchandise and cash. As they went, they added to their plan. For example, if the crew of the captured ship was too large to murder right away, Rachel would lure some of them back onto her ship by asking them to help her fix a leak. This divided the crew into two smaller crews, who could be killed in two phases: one on the Walls's boat, and one on the crew's boat. Not only did the Walls make a lot of money doing this, but they also had all the fish they could eat.

In September 1782, the pirates' lucky streak ended. They were headed out to sea—presumably to commit another robbery—when the storm became much wilder than predicted. In the squall, all crew members except Rachel were swept overboard and drowned. In an ironic twist of fate, after the storm Rachel found herself on the deck weeping and wailing for a rescue, but this time her distress was real. She was eventually picked up and taken back to Boston. Did the ship's captain who picked her up suspect that the poor, half-drowned woman he was ferrying home was actually a bloodthirsty pirate with a knack for killing kindly captains? He was probably not even aware that such a pirate existed. After all, Rachel and her pirates did not leave any survivors, and dead men tell no tales.

Back in Boston, now a widow, Rachel was hired again as a maid. She was done with seafaring piracy, but she had not given up her lawbreaking ways. More than once she snuck down to the waterfront to pilfer ships at anchor. Always clever, she targeted the captain's quarters as a place where precious goods would be hidden. She was never caught for these robberies, and she amassed a sizable amount of loot.

In 1789, seven years after she left the pirate life, she was arrested for stopping a woman on the road and stealing her bonnet, worth seven shillings. For this crime—and this crime only—she was sentenced to death. Until the very end, she proclaimed her innocence in this particular crime. She gave an extraordinary last confession where she admitted to her long career as a thief. She refused to admit to the robbery that would cost her her life, but she detailed a number of other crimes, including the pilfering of the ships at the docks. She also exonerated a woman for a crime that she herself had committed, expressing sadness that the other woman had suffered a long punishment for the crime. She did not mention her life as a pirate, and she claimed that she did not know where her husband was at the time of her imprisonment. She *did* mention that she had committed too many crimes to list, and that she did not desire to make her confession too long. Rachel did not write out the entire account of her life of crime, but she mentioned that she confessed each one to God (and presumably her priest) and hoped for his forgiveness. She also said that she hoped that her life would prove a "solemn warning and caution" to everyone, but especially to women.

Rachel Wall was executed on October 7, 1789. She was the last woman to be hanged by the state of Massachusetts.

DEATH PENALTY IN MASSACHUSETTS

Although Rachel Wall was the last woman to be hanged in Massachusetts, she was certainly not the only one. The Massachusetts Bay Colony, and eventually the state of Massachusetts, executed 345 people—women and men—from its founding in 1628 to its abolition of the death penalty in 1984.

Many of the earliest hangings were victims of the Puritans. Although they themselves had come to America in search of religious freedom, they did not offer that same freedom to people who were not Puritans, such as Quakers. Four Quakers in particular, Mary Dyer, Marmaduke Stephenson, William Robinson, and William Leddra, are known as the Boston martyrs because of their hangings, which occurred from 1659 to 1661.

The Salem Witch trials, which took place in Salem, Massachusetts, resulted in 19 hangings and 1 death by torture during the years 1692 and 1693. The city of Boston hanged three women found guilty of witchcraft. Many pirates were also hanged in Boston, including the six surviving crew members of the *Whydah*, the world's only authenticated pirate shipwreck, in 1717.

In Boston, people were hanged on the Great Elm, called the oldest citizen of Boston. This tree stood long before the English arrived in Boston, and it lived until 1876, when it was demolished in a storm. Many people met their deaths on this tree, which served as a hanging spot until 1769. Rachel was hanged 20 years too late to die on the elm and would have been hanged publicly on the gallows instead.

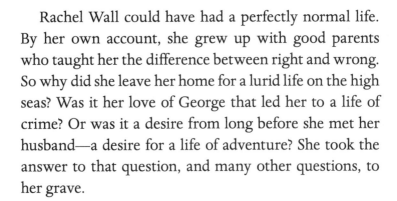

Rachel Wall could have had a perfectly normal life. By her own account, she grew up with good parents who taught her the difference between right and wrong. So why did she leave her home for a lurid life on the high seas? Was it her love of George that led her to a life of crime? Or was it a desire from long before she met her husband—a desire for a life of adventure? She took the answer to that question, and many other questions, to her grave.

Learn More

Druett, Joan. *She Captains: Heroines and Hellions of the Sea*. New York: Simon and Schuster, 2000.

Life, Last Words and Dying Confession, of Rachel Wall: Who, with William Smith and William Dunogan, Were Executed at Boston, on Thursday, October 8, 1789, for High-way Robbery (Boston printed broadside).

Sadie Farrell

Many children like adventure stories. Tales of knights, dragons, ninjas, wizards, and even pirates inspire and entertain, allowing readers to live out fantasies they might never encounter in real life. Usually, these stories are put aside as people grow and the wild legends of youth are forgotten. Dreams of magic and adventure become dreams of wealth and status, and the need for wizards and pirates lessens.

For Sadie Farrell, that need did not fade as she grew up. Her thirst for adventure was so great that she carried her favorite childhood stories to adulthood and brought them to life. She was not content just to imagine being a pirate from a story; she became one.

Sadie's life story comes from one main published source, Herbert Asbury's 1928 book *Gangs of New York:*

An Informal History of the Underworld. Someone as successful as Sadie allegedly was should have appeared in the local newspapers, if not in the police records, but she does not. It is possible that she never existed—at least not exactly as the stories tell it. But it is also possible that she simply was never caught, or her crimes were attributed to someone else, such as a male counterpart. Still, her legend looms large in New York history, and she deserves her place among more verified pirates, if only because she would be so absolutely thrilled to be there.

Sadie was born during the mid-1800s and grew up poor among the pickpockets and other criminals of Manhattan's Lower East Side in the Fourth Ward. New York City at that time was a powder keg of too many mistreated immigrants and too little space that was constantly erupting into violence. America, land of immigrants, sometimes gave cold welcome to the "new" immigrants of this period, who were needed to labor in the mills and factories. Earlier immigrants depended on the new immigrants' labor but still resented them for the foreign ideas and cultures they brought from home. Although today the Lower East side is the home of trendy, upscale shops and condos, in Sadie's day it was full of "ramshackle tenements [which housed] a miserable population steeped in vice and poverty," according to Asbury. Instead of the police, gangs ruled the streets. The worst of them were the gangs of the Fourth Ward, which was where Sadie got her start.

BOSS TWEED

Not all criminals are as easy to spot as pirates are. One of New York's most notorious crooks wore a business suit and the air of a respectable gentleman. His name was William M. "Boss" Tweed, and he used kindness to immigrants as a tool to fleece New York City out of $25 million.

Tweed started out in politics as an alderman but rose quickly through the ranks until 1868, when he was virtually running the entire city through his cronies and his "Tweed ring." He chose who was elected to every post in the city, and once someone was elected, he chose how they voted. He ran bribery schemes, sent outrageously inflated construction bills to the city, and ran fake leases on his vast real estate holdings. If there was an illegal way to make money, Boss Tweed was probably doing it.

Tweed got away with his crimes for so long because of the tremendous loyalty he inspired, mainly in Irish Catholic immigrants. He was seen as a benevolent figure by the immigrant communities, organizing picnics and functions for children as well as helping people navigate America's bureaucracy and customs. In return, all Tweed required was a vote for the person he endorsed. People yearning for any small kindness in an unfriendly country flocked to Tweed and did what he asked, no questions asked.

Eventually, Tweed was brought down by journalists and political cartoonists who turned the public against him. He was tried and convicted of forgery and larceny in 1873.

Sadie grew up around violence. As a teen, she would have witnessed the New York City draft riot firsthand. During the Civil War, New Yorkers fed up with the loss of life and the new mandatory draft burned down buildings and bridges, tore up railroad tracks, and unleashed mayhem (much of it against the black people of the city) for four whole days—the bloodiest urban insurrection in American history. She also saw the daily violence that went on around her in the bloody Fourth Ward, especially on Water Street, the scene of "more violent crime than any other street on the continent." The sailors who populated the waterfront bars did not know the area well and were often drunk, making them perfect robbery victims. A clever thief could have her pick of the nearly endless prospects.

Sadie was just such a clever thief. She was small but scrappy. She learned how to disarm her opponents without fighting them hand-to-hand, where she would almost certainly lose. Instead, she used the element of surprise, head-butting a man in the stomach, knocking the wind out of him. Her male partner would then knock the guy out and rob him. This method earned her the nickname Sadie the Goat. Sadie made a living by robbing people. She had a small income but a large reputation. She must have made more than a few enemies during her time on the street, but only one major enemy is known.

Gallus Mag, so called for her habit of wearing men's trousers and suspenders (called galluses) was the co-owner of the Hole in the Wall pub. She was a six-foot-tall

English woman who, besides being co-owner, was also the bouncer of the bar. Mag was a savage woman, and even the police were afraid of her. She was known for biting the ears off people who crossed her, and she kept those ears in a jar on top of the bar for all to see. One night in the spring of 1869, Sadie got into a fight with Mag that cost her an ear. The women's rivalry was so well known that Sadie's ear got a special jar all its own, with Sadie's name on it. Sadie left the bar humiliated, determined to find a new bar and possibly a new job.

Sadie walked a long way after her fight with Mag, leaving her territory and crossing into the west side of the city, near New York Harbor. As luck would have it, she walked by right as the Charlton Street Gang, a small-time gang with their headquarters in an old gin mill at the foot of Charlton Street, clumsily attempted to capture a ship floating down the North (present day Hudson) River. Their pathetic efforts were easily overpowered by the ship's crew, and they were kicked off the ship immediately.

To Sadie, this was a sign. Robbing people one at a time was all right, but robbing an entire ship would be so much better. Surely the best career for her was a pirate's life! Still bleeding heavily from her lost ear, Sadie approached the gang and convinced them that they needed a new leader. If they let Sadie take over, she would lead them to more successful attempts at plundering. The Charlton Street boys agreed, and a new crew of pirates was born. Within a week they had captured

TREASURE ISLAND

One book is responsible for nearly all the pirate stereotypes spread through the ages. When Robert Louis Stevenson sat down to dash off a simple adventure story for boys, even he scarcely could have imagined the long-term financial and cultural success his book would enjoy. Written in less than a month, this enduring classic captured the public's imagination in 1881 and has not let go of it since.

The book tells the story of young Jim Hawkins, an innkeeper's son, who is swept up in a wild adventure when pirate Billy Bones comes into the tavern one night, raving about a one-legged man and the black spot and holding a treasure map. A wealthy Englishman, Squire Trelawney, hires Jim as a cabin boy on the voyage to track down the treasure on Billy Bones's map, treasure that belonged to Captain Flint before he died. The luckless Trelawney hires many of Flint's former pirate crew to sail on his ship, and he is mutinied upon. The pirates and the Englishmen cross and double-cross each other, each side attempting to be the first to the treasure. In the end, the "good guys" get the treasure, the pirates are vanquished, and young Jim returns home much wealthier than when he left it.

Throughout the story, one pirate stands out: Long John Silver, ship's cook and pirate. No one is ever truly safe around Silver because his allegiances change quickly and his smooth talking conceals his true intent.

The mysterious yet alluring pirate who hides deadly intent behind a smile and a clever word would serve as a model for many pirates that came after, including *Pirates of the Caribbean*'s Captain Jack Sparrow. With Long John Silver, Stevenson invented the "pirate with a heart of gold . . . sort of" that has been at the center of every good pirate yarn since then.

In a way, Stevenson didn't just create a good pirate story, he also created the character of pirate with a capital *P*. Long John Silver is, believe it or not, not even *Treasure Island*'s most enduring legacy. The ideas of walking the plank, buried treasure, and even "X marks the spot" all were popularized in this children's story.

a boat, hoisted the Jolly Roger, and set sail up the river, searching for treasure.

Nobody knows where Sadie learned to sail. River navigation is not nearly as difficult as ocean navigation, but she would have needed at least some skill to pilot her ship up and down the river. It is possible that some of the Charlton Street boys had more sailing skills than pirating know-how and were able to teach Sadie. Maybe she absorbed sailing technique from all the pirate stories she read as a young girl. It is unknown which pirate stories Sadie was familiar with or where she first encountered them, but she definitely had a working knowledge of pirate lore. She copied the stories of pirates in many aspects.

THE JOLLY ROGER

When Sadie strung up a black flag with a skull and crossbones, she probably did not realize that the "pirate flag" had only recently been selected as *the* pirate flag. In the 1700s, many pirates flew flags that were specific to them instead of a uniform flag. The flags could be red, black, or even green, with some combination of symbols for time, death, and violence.

The black with skull and crossbones (or crossed swords) design is attributed to a few different pirates, mainly Sam Bellamy and Calico Jack Rackham, although nobody knows who first flew the flag that would become the standard pirate flag. Pirate flags were meant to convey the message that death was imminent if the pirates were not obeyed quickly. Their purpose was strike fear into the hearts of law-abiding sailors, and they worked very well.

The name *Jolly Roger* first appeared in the 1720s. Some say that it was an Anglicization of the French words *jolie rouge*, which mean "pretty red." (The French were known to fly red pirate flags.) Others dispute this and believe the flag's name comes from a nickname for the devil, Old Roger. However the name came about, by the 1730s it referred to a black flag with a skull and crossbones, which remains the symbol for pirates to this day.

For example, she is one of the few known pirates to have made their victims walk the plank. Sadie was a real pirate who lived the life of a fantasy pirate—one of the strangest examples of the American dream ever imagined.

For a while, everything went well. Under Sadie's guidance, the Charlton Street Gang was able to raid several villages and houses up the Hudson River as far north as Poughkeepsie, a distance of over 80 miles. They knew the richest target they could attack would be the seaport itself, but it was too heavily guarded for them to stand a chance at winning.

Sadie wasn't interested in going out in a blaze of glory. She wanted two things: to make money and to live long enough to spend it. The pirates tried their luck at large commercial ocean steamers, but the ships were too much for their small operation to handle. What they excelled at was stealing small, valuable items from mansions along the river and less-guarded ships. Once they had the valuables, they were able to fence, or resell, their stolen goods to various pawnshops back in Manhattan. No doubt Sadie's previous life as a pickpocket had introduced her to several shady pawnbrokers who didn't ask too many questions.

Sadie and her pirates made a good amount of money in this way. Police Chief George W. Matsell described their methods like this: "The river pirates pursue their nefarious operations with the most systematic perseverance, and manifest a shrewdness and adroitness which can only be attained by long practice. . . . In their boats, under cover of night, they prowl around the wharves and vessels in a stream, and dexterously snatch up every piece of loose property left for a moment unguarded."

Eventually, the landowners who lived on the river's edge decided they had endured enough and banded together against Sadie and her boys. Farmers started to greet Sadie's arrival with guns, and a seaborne police force put a stop to her ship-robbing practice.

Sadie realized that the game had gotten too dangerous to be profitable. She and her remaining crewmembers abandoned their little ship and returned to her old stomping grounds of the Fourth Ward underworld. Sadie's time as a pirate had done her good—she was now hailed as Queen of the Waterfront. So lofty was her new status that she decided to return to the Hole in the Wall bar. She apologized to Mag for her part in the fight they had. Mag, who was either moved by Sadie's generosity of spirit or impressed by her courage at walking into the bar policed by Manhattan's fiercest bouncer, returned Sadie's ear to her. Sadie allegedly wore this ear in a locket around her neck for the rest of her days.

What happened to Sadie after the meeting with Gallus Mag is unknown. A happy version of events claims that she opened her own bar with the profits she made from her pirating exploits. In other stories, she just fades into obscurity, disappearing into the pages of history. Perhaps she was murdered in an alley by some young thief who was clueless about her legendary pedigree. Stranger things have happened in the Fourth Ward.

No matter how she eventually died—or even if she ever lived—Sadie lives on today. The South Street Seaport Museum in New York City offers a walking tour that features Sadie's exploits. She appears in some form in at least four novels. There is even a character based on Sadie in the Martin Scorsese film *Gangs of New York*.

Asbury's account of Sadie paints a mixed picture. He seems fond of her but does not present her as particularly competent or frightening. (He reserves his most effusive praise for Gallus Mag, who seems much more dangerous than Sadie.) Still, Asbury does insist that Sadie provided "inspired leadership" that "breathed new life" into the gang, and that her "ferocity far exceeded that of her ruffianly followers," so he does not entirely write her off as a foolish girl. If anything, he seems unsure of what to make of her—a problem potentially shared with many readers. Who was this woman who wasn't afraid to go toe-to-toe with murderous criminals yet still had enough whimsy to fly a Jolly Roger? If she existed, it is a shame that her life was not recorded more carefully.

Sadie is the last known American female pirate. As the 20th century began, American pirates moved inland and became captains of industry and progress, more like Boss Tweed than Long John Silver. But her adventurous spirit—and the American dream—are still going strong today. Her life, inspired by legend, is now itself a story that emboldens people to seek out adventure. She would have approved of becoming a part of the legends that she loved. Who will be the next legend to draw inspiration from Sadie?

Learn More

Asbury, Herbert. *Gangs of New York: An Informal History of the Underworld*. Reprint ed. New York: Vintage, 2008.

Bernstein, Iver. "July 13–16, 1863: The New York City Draft Riots." *Civil War Times* 42, no. 3 (August 2003).

Daniels, Roger. *Coming to America: A History of Immigration and Ethnicity in American Life*. 2nd ed. New York: Harper Perennial, 2002.

Anne Bonny

Of all the known female pirates, Anne Bonny is the most famous. Her name and exploits feature in so many pirate stories that she has become the archetype of a pirate woman. When people conjure up an image of a female pirate, they probably think of one who looks like Anne Bonny. So how did this pirate become *the* female pirate, despite not being a pirate for very long or having much success?

Anne Bonny was a wild woman. Her fearlessness and her desire for adventure were stronger than most other people's, male or female. From her childhood, she chafed at the confines of her life and reached for adventure in any way she could. Her love of adventure shaped her destiny and made her a pirate who is beloved the world over, long after her death.

From her birth, Anne's life was marked for chaos. Her father, William Cormac, was a wealthy and prominent lawyer in Cork, Ireland. Her mother was not his wife, Mrs. Cormac, but the family's housekeeper, Peggy. The affair between William and his maid caused a large scandal that cost Anne's father many of his legal clients. Without clients, he had no way to make money and was forced to ask his wife for an allowance to live on. He knew that even if his estranged wife would be kind enough to support him, she would never support his illegitimate daughter, so he came up with a plan. He dressed Anne as a boy and claimed that she was a relative's child whom he was training to be his legal apprentice.

For a while this worked, and William, Peggy, and Anne lived off the money sent by Mrs. Cormac. Eventually, though, William's wife figured out that his "nephew" was actually his illegitimate daughter and cut them all off. Penniless, William had no choice but to move to a place where his past was unknown. If he could set up a business again, free from his past scandal, his new family would have a chance of survival. William, Peggy, and their daughter set off for America in search of a new start.

William changed careers and became a merchant in the Carolina colony. He and his family settled in present-day South Carolina and enjoyed even more wealth than they had back in Ireland. William eventually became the owner of a large plantation. After her mother died, Anne became mistress of this plantation at just 12 years old. As soon as she was in charge of the house, everyone was subject to her fiery temper.

There are many legends about Anne's behavior during her plantation days. She was said to punish her servants severely for disobedience, going so far as to stab one with a knife. Her violence was not just for the hired help, either. When a suitor tried to put his hands on her, she beat him so severely that he was laid up for weeks. Her father did not encourage this behavior but could do little to curb it.

Anne ruled the plantation unchecked until she refused her father's demand that she marry a suitable eligible bachelor. A pretty daughter of a wealthy merchant would have had her pick of husbands, but Anne rejected all of the qualified candidates. She chose instead the poor, small-time sailor James Bonny, which both enraged her father and broke his heart. He disowned her, and she ran off, never to set eyes on her father again. A legend claims she retaliated against her father by setting his plantation on fire, although this was never proven.

The newlyweds set off toward the untamed Caribbean. It was at that time a place where people with few morals and fewer fears could make a lot of money, if they were smart. Woodes Rogers, the new governor of the Bahamas, declared he would pay good money to anyone who turned in a pirate, no questions asked. James thought that he would try his luck as a pirate hunter. Captain Charles Johnson says in *The General History of the Pyrates* that James was disappointed Anne had been disinherited, making it seem that perhaps James had courted her only for her fortune. Anne and her new husband sailed to New Providence, Bahamas, straight into the last hurrah of the Golden Age of Piracy.

THE GOLDEN AGE

In the early days of the 18th century, pirates outnumbered law-abiding citizens two to one in the Bahamas. Never before (and not since) had so many pirates been active in such a concentrated area. By Anne Bonny's time, the pirates had migrated to New Providence to make their final stand. They conducted business in the thriving black market there, trading liquor, slaves, and other stolen items. They bought, sold, and repaired their ships and weaponry. They also whiled away the off-duty hours in the taverns and brothels of the island, eating and drinking their way through a month's pay in one night. It was a wild place full of wild people who lived like they'd live forever. But the end of the Golden Age was coming much sooner than any of them could guess.

Woodes Rogers was appointed governor of the Bahamas in 1717. His goal: to end the pirate menace. England wanted the Bahamas to be a respectable and profitable colony, and to make that happen Rogers needed the pirates to leave. Many governors before him had made half-hearted attempts to curb piracy, but Rogers was relentless in his pursuit of them. His decree that all pirates who surrendered would be pardoned sent a clear message: give up, or die fighting.

Rogers executed many pirates and did bring an end to the pirates' reign over the Bahamas, but he could not make the island prosperous and eventually ended up serving time in debtors' prison. Today he is surely rolling in his grave, because the Bahamas is enjoying prosperity because of tourists, many of them seeking pirate haunts and hideouts.

James's pirate hunting business took him to various pirate hot spots around the island. Anne sometimes visited them as well. On one of her forays, Anne met the man who became the love of her life, John Rackham. This small-time pirate, known as Calico Jack, fell deeply in love with the Irish woman. According to a historical account, he wooed her as he sailed, "no time wasted, straight up alongside, every gun brought to play, and the prize boarded." By all accounts, the feeling was mutual and the pair would remain together until death parted them. When James discovered his wife's affair, Calico Jack offered to buy Anne from him in a "divorce by purchase," but James refused, asking Governor Rogers to instead enforce an old law and publicly whip Anne for adultery. This request was Jack and Anne's first brush with Woodes Rogers, but it would not be the last. The lovers fled Anne's punishment and sailed toward safer seas.

How and when Anne joined Jack's crew is unknown. Perhaps when she boarded his ship she knew she was going to be part of his pirating career, but she may have been simply seeking refuge from the lash. Maybe when her eyes first met Jack's in a crowded tavern, she had already chosen the life of a pirate for herself.

No matter when Anne officially became a pirate, she definitely did so and was a part of Jack's crew by the summer of 1720 at the latest. At some point during her travels, she bore Jack a child, who was born in Cuba. What happened to the baby is unclear. Some accounts say the baby died, others claim that it was given up for adoption. Who knows—today in Cuba there may be descendants of the most famous pirate power couple of all time who aren't even aware of their heritage. After Anne delivered the baby, she rejoined Jack and the crew and resumed pirating.

JACK RACKHAM

Like many pirates, Jack Rackham's early life is mostly unknown. He was born during the end of the 17th century somewhere in England. His first appearance in history was as the quartermaster (second in command) under Captain Charles Vane.

In November 1718, Vane decided not to pursue a French ship, much to the dismay of his crew. During battle a captain's word is absolute and nobody can disobey, but once the fighting was over, the dissatisfied crew voted to remove Charles Vane from his captaincy and elected Jack Rackham instead. This level of democracy, with each crew member getting a vote of equal status and being able to elect new leaders at will, was unheard of in the navy ships of the time. This type of liberty was one of the many reasons that scores of seamen left the Royal Navy for a pirate's life.

Once Rackham took over Vane's ship, he gained a reputation as a gentleman pirate who wasn't interested in torturing or murdering his victims. There are several accounts of him making an effort to return ships and passengers home safely after he plundered their treasure. He was never highly successful and did not quite measure up to his contemporaries like Blackbeard. Were it not for his association with Anne Bonny and Mary Read, it is likely he would have disappeared from history altogether.

Around the same time that Anne rejoined Rackham, the crew picked up a new sailor from a merchant ship they captured. The slim fellow, Mark Read, was really Mary Read—a woman who had long dressed and passed as a man on the high seas. (Mary's story is in part II, "Escape.") Anne and "Mark" became fast friends, and eventually "Mark" revealed to Anne that *he* was actually *she*. Rackham, jealous that Anne had been spending so much time with the handsome "Mark," was also informed of Read's gender.

Whether or not the rest of the crew was aware is a matter up for debate. Captain Johnson's account claims that the crew never knew Mary was a woman, but testimony at trial proves that their victims, at least, were well aware that Anne and Mary were women. Captives testified that the women "were very active on Board and willing to do any Thing . . . they did not seem to be kept or detained by Force, but of their own Free-Will and Consent." Another witness testified that "[the women] were both very profligate, cursing and swearing much, and very ready and willing to do any Thing on board." In light of this, it seems strange that Johnson would say that Anne and Mary's fellow crew never discovered they were women. Maybe Johnson didn't want to discuss why, if the crew knew that Anne and Mary were women, they did not reject their presence on board. Nevertheless, Anne, Jack, and Mary sailed together on Rackham's ship during the summer and fall of 1720 and had many pirating successes during that time.

Their biggest win was the theft of the sloop *William* in August 1720. This 12-ton sloop was a British warship that could hold up to 18 guns. It was not particularly large for a British warship, but it was a large ship for the pirates. For the pirates, the most thrilling thing about this particular theft was the fact that they stole it right from Nassau's harbor—a direct signal to Governor Woodes Rogers that they were not afraid of him or his authority (even on his home turf).

This bold action spelled the beginning of the end for the band of pirates. On September 5, 1720, Woodes

Rogers made a proclamation that Jack and his crew, including "two women, by name, Anne Fulford alias Bonny & Mary Read," were enemies to the Crown of Great Britain. He dispatched pirate hunter John Barnet to capture them and set the clock ticking toward their end.

The pirates were captured on October 22, 1720. Captain Barnet came across the pirates at Negril Point, Jamaica. Once he confirmed who they were, he ordered their immediate surrender. Legend has it that the pirate crew was below deck sleeping and playing cards when the surrender order came, and only Anne and Mary were on deck keeping watch. When the women realized that they were under attack, they bellowed into the hold to rouse the men, but none came to help. Mary Read is rumored to have fired her gun in an attempt to get her fellow crew members moving, wounding several of her fellow crew.

While the men, including Captain Rackham, cowered down below, Anne and Mary fought off their attackers like ferocious beasts. With swords and pistols, they held off Barnet's men for an admirably long time, even taking some of them down, but eventually the two women were overpowered and the ship was taken. Anne, Mary, and the rest of the crew were taken to Jamaica for their trials.

The High Court of Admiralty assembled in Spanish Town, Jamaica, on November 16, 1720. All of Rackham's men were tried. A few who convinced the court that they had been press-ganged into service were acquitted, but the majority of the men were convicted as pirates and sentenced to hang. One of the first to face the noose was Captain Jack Rackham. His body was displayed publicly as a warning to would-be pirates and as a statement of Rogers's authority. The spot where his body hung as it decayed, near the entrance to Port Royal Harbor, is still known as Rackham's Cay.

Before he was to be executed, Jack asked for one last moment with his beloved to say goodbye. Knowing Anne as he did, he was likely not expecting tears or sweet words of comfort from her. However, even he was probably not expecting her last words to him to be that she was "sorry to see him there, but if he had fought like a Man, he need not have been hang'd like a Dog." Hopefully he went to his death smiling, knowing that not even the threat of death could subdue the fiery woman he loved.

Ten days after Jack's execution, on November 28, 1720, Anne and Mary were tried for piracy. They were not accused of murder, but of "Piracies, Felonies, and Robberies . . . on the High Sea," which was punishable by death. Both women pled not guilty. Numerous people testified that the women were active participants in the business of piracy and had as much guilt as their male coworkers did. The women said very little throughout the trial and did not give statements in their own defense, though they were given the opportunity to do so. It was not until they were both sentenced to death that Anne and Mary announced to the court that they were pregnant. Each was examined by a doctor and found to be pregnant, and so Anne's and Mary's sentences were commuted until after their babies were born. These women could not escape the noose, but they could postpone it. The court was determined that innocent children would not be killed, but it was apparently not bothered by the fact that by condemning these women to death, these innocent children would be forced to grow up without their mothers.

Mary Read did not live to see the gallows. She died in prison in 1721, either in childbirth or from a type of typhus called "prison fever." What happened to Anne Bonny is even more of a mystery. There are no official records of her death in prison, her execution, or the birth of her baby. Some accounts claim that her wealthy and influential father secured a pardon for her at the last minute and whisked her back to Carolina, where she married a gentleman and lived out her days as a law-abiding citizen. Other stories suggest that she escaped. A particularly fanciful tale says that Bartholomew Roberts, another feared and famous pirate of the time, broke her out of jail and asked her to join his crew. She may have also returned to her birth country of Ireland. Wherever she ended her days, one hopes that she did it on her own terms, living her life in the way she thought was best. Anne would probably have been happier to die alone in prison than warm in her bed at home, married to a man she did not love.

It is fitting that the circumstances of Anne's death are not known, because that makes it easier to pretend that she never died. Indeed, her legend lives on in pirate novels, movies, and TV shows, notably in the recent Starz series *Black Sails*. Her lust for adventure led her to live a rough and dangerous life. It must not have been an easy life, but it was the life she chose for herself.

Women today may not understand her choice to sail with lawless men, but they very likely *can* understand her desire for more out of life than she was offered. Anne took her destiny into her own hands and ensured that her legend will continue to live on as long as there are women who dream of adventure.

Learn More

Defoe, Daniel. *A General History of the Pyrates*. Mineola, New York: Dover Maritime, 1999.

Konstam, Angus, and David Rickman. *Pirate: The Golden Age*. Oxford: Osprey Publishing, 2011.

Sherry, Frank. *Raiders and Rebels: The Golden Age of Piracy*. Reprint ed. New York: Harper Perennial, 2008.

Woodard, Colin. *Republic of Pirates: Being the True and Surprising Story of the Caribbean Pirates and the Man Who Brought Them Down*. Boston: Mariner Books, 2008.

Part V
POWER

Lady Mary Killigrew

When most little girls dream of marriage, they imagine the wedding itself more than the groom. If they do imagine a groom, many girls think of a man who is similar to their father—often the most important man in their life up to that point.

Mary Wolverston was a girl who married a man just like her father. Mary's father was a pirate, and Mary learned from him what a pirate's life could be. When she grew up, she chose a pirate for her husband so that she could become a pirate and share in the power that piracy brought. When Mary wed Sir John Killigrew, she made her dreams come true. As Lady Mary Killigrew, she enjoyed the refined, gracious life that was customary for a lord and lady, and she also enjoyed the power and money that were customary for notorious pirates. Her position as lady of a fine home allowed her to manage a pirate empire right under the law's nose. She had so much power, masked by her nobility, that it took an authority figure no less powerful than Queen Elizabeth I to finally take her down.

Mary Wolverston was born in Wolverston Hall in Suffolk, England, in the early 1500s. She was the daughter of Philip Wolverston, who was known as a "gentleman pirate." King Henry VIII's break with Catholicism caused England to fall out of favor with much of Europe, which was predominantly Catholic at the time. Doing legitimate business with every country but Germany (which was emerging as Protestant) became difficult, so trade had to happen illegitimately—by pirates. Wealthy landowners who lived by the water found themselves able to offer seafaring pirates a place to land, money to bribe officials, and help in selling their off-the-books cargo, all for a price of course. Mary's father was one of these gentleman pirates, and his work made quite an impression on his daughter.

After a childhood spent observing the workings of a pirate household, Mary got one for herself. She married Sir John Killigrew IV sometime in the late 1550s or early 1560s. It is easy to see why they wed: his land holdings were vast and his political connections were strong, which was a perfect pedigree for a gentleman pirate. Her husband was the vice admiral of Cornwall, the royal governor of Pendennis Castle, lord of his own Arwenack Manor, and a blood relation of Queen Elizabeth's minister William Cecil, Lord Burleigh. His pirating career was already in full swing by the time

PIRACY: A FAMILY AFFAIR

The Killigrews are not the only family whose family business was piracy. Many pirate women entered the pirate life through a family member, often a male family member. The family member's presence might have helped the women gain acceptance in the pirate community and overcome the prejudices associated with women onboard a ship. Looking at it this way, it makes the women who became pirates on their own even more remarkable.

Besides Mary Killigrew, who grew up with a pirate father and married a pirate husband, there were other women who joined the pirate ranks due to a family member. For example, Grace O'Malley entered piracy through her father. She followed him to sea at a young age and eventually surpassed him in pirating skill. Maria Cobham, Rachel Wall, Margaret Jordan, and Cheng I Sao all married into the pirate trade. Maria Cobham and Cheng I Sao are notable for both becoming much greater pirates than either of their husbands were. Cheng I Sao, in particular, went on to claim the title of the most successful pirate of all time, male or female, after her husband's death. No matter how women came to piracy, the evidence suggests that once they arrived there, they flourished.

he wed Mary, and she merged seamlessly into the family business.

Whether the couple shared love or even affection is unknown, but they definitely shared their pirate work with each other. The newlywed Killigrews, along with his mother Lady Elizabeth Killigrew (born Elizabeth Trewinnard), ran a bustling pirate business from Arwenack Manor. Many historical sources confuse Lady Elizabeth and Lady Mary, which is an easy mistake given that both of them shared the last name Killigrew by marriage and both were involved in the family's piratical business. While they were both pirates, Lady Mary took a much more active role in piracy than her mother-in-law did. Regardless, it is intriguing that there are multiple women to choose from in this particular pirate empire.

Philip Gosse, author of *The History of Piracy*, calls the Killigrew family a "veritable oligarchy of corsair capitalists." The Killigrews did not often participate in the actual pirate raids and voyages themselves, although Mary used her husband's frequent absences for business as an excuse to take a more hands-on approach to piracy than her husband. Besides sailing, the family handled every other aspect of the pirating business. If someone needed to find a fast, maneuverable ship, he went to the Killigrews to find one. When someone needed money to bribe an official, she asked the Killigrews for a loan. If a crew had a dispute about how they were paid, they knew to appeal to the Killigrews to intervene. The family was a "one-stop shop" if one wanted to outfit a pirate venture. Their home in Arwenack Manor served as their base of operations. There, they assessed the stolen goods to make sure they were valued correctly before they were sold. Their respected family name and fancy house were excellent covers for their shady dealings. Few suspected that the sweet lady (and mother of five, no less) and noble lord were notorious outlaws.

For all of their many services, the Killigrews collected a hefty fee, and Queen Elizabeth received her share of it as well. Piracy was illegal, officially, so the queen could not condone it, but she relied on and depended on her pirates, just as her father King Henry VIII had before her. Piracy brought home the money that was the lifeblood of the fledgling British Empire. Who cared if it was illegal? Certainly not the queen nor the Killigrew family. Both grew wealthy off piratical proceeds.

~~~~~~~~~~~~~~~~~~~~~~~~

THE QUEEN'S PIRATES

Queen Elizabeth I's reign boasts its fair share of accomplishments: the creation of a British national identity, an outpouring of theatrical drama by William Shakespeare and his contemporaries, and the defeat of the Spanish Armada, among others. What history usually leaves out is her heavy reliance on an unconventional task force to accomplish her goals: the pirates.

Good Queen Bess secretly employed many pirates, known as her "sea dogs," to increase England's treasury. Many of them went on to become England's most celebrated heroes. Sir Francis Drake, later famous for circumnavigating the world by sea, got his start by sailing for England as a privateer. He first sailed as a slave trader, but after he was attacked by Spaniards in Mexico, he turned to Spanish destruction. As a pirate employed by Queen Elizabeth, he carried out a very successful raid on the Spanish stronghold Nombre de Dios. He also took several Spanish treasure ships, one—*Senora de la Conception*—massive enough to earn him his knighthood. He, along with fellow English pirate John Hawkins, sailed against the Spanish Armada and proved essential to its defeat in 1588.

Sir John Hawkins, another privateer, was a master shipbuilder as well. His improvements to ship designs helped launch England as a world power. Before Hawkins, ships fought by ramming into each other. Hawkins understood that the new invention of the long-range cannon would change that, so he equipped the English warship with cannons to give it the advantage in long-range battles. Without his foresight and ingenuity, the Spanish Armada may not have been defeated by the English. The world today could look unimaginably different than it does had Spain's "invincible armada" triumphed over England, but they did not prevail, thanks to one of Queen Elizabeth's most favorite pirates. For his service to England, which would only become more impressive with the passage of time, Queen Elizabeth knighted him in 1588.

The Killigrew family had, if not an official arrangement, then an understanding with the queen. She looked the other way while pirates regularly sailed in and out of Falmouth Harbor where the Killigrews lived. If not for Lady Mary's wildest piratical adventure, the Killigrew family might have gone on pirating for as long as they pleased. But one of Lady Mary's escapades nearly cost the family their pirate business and Lady Mary her life.

In 1582, a Hanseatic ship sailed into Falmouth Harbor near Arwenack Manor. Due to unexpected foul weather, the ship was forced to drop anchor and seek shelter on land for its crew. It would be too dangerous to try to ride out the storm onboard the ship, so two men were sent ashore to find food and a place to stay. These two men, Philip de Orozo and Juan de Charis, could scarcely believe their good fortune to find Arwenack Manor, home to such a noble and generous hostess as Lady Mary. She probably served the sailors tea in front of a roaring fireplace while she listened to their story. She reassured them that their ship would of course be safe in the harbor until the storm blew over and that the crew could room at a guest house nearby.

The gentlemen were set at ease by the woman's hospitality and the knowledge that the Hanseatic League and England were at peace. They took her at her word, left the ship in the harbor with only a few crew members onboard, and set off for the guest house.

THE HANSEATIC LEAGUE

In the middle ages, a small group of merchant and navy ships and ports grew to be one of the largest anti-piracy forces on the water. The Hanseatic League was a group of guilds and towns that stretched from the North Sea to the Baltic Sea. The league functioned like a union that protected the economic and diplomatic rights of its members in the ports and towns that made up the league. It wasn't an official state or even a city-state, but it held lots of power during its existence, especially during its height in the 1400s. The league was made up of parts of modern-day Poland, Estonia, Belgium, Germany, and other countries.

The league's monopoly on sea trade made them a natural fit to become the "pirate police," as they spent so much time on the water. With the help of the navies and monies of the league's port towns, the league made it very hard for pirates in the area to find a safe place to dock their ships, sell their goods, or hide from the authorities. The league's trademark ship, the cog, was an oak-made, single-rudder ship featuring a single square-rigged sail. The design was copied by many countries and eventually became the standard model for both sailing ships and warships. The cog is perhaps the Hanseatic League's greatest lasting legacy.

Lady Mary examined the Hanseatic ship by spyglass as soon as her guests left her parlor. She decided that she should have such a handsome ship for herself. She was well into middle age at this point, but she was still young enough for a dangerous caper. She gathered a crew of her own, including two of her household servants, and sailed out to the league ship that night, wrapping her oars in cloth to muffle their sound. The makeshift crew climbed aboard and loaded the treasure and goods from the ship onto their own smaller ship. A skeleton crew of the Killigrew party (not including Lady Mary) sailed the Hanseatic ship out of the harbor all the way up to Ireland, where it could be hidden. When de Orozo and de Charis returned to the harbor once the skies were clear, only seagulls marked the spot where their 144-ton ship had been.

The furious men immediately suspected foul play. The storm had not been bad enough to sink the ship, and there was no evidence in the harbor to indicate that it had gone down. Someone must have taken it maliciously. De Orozo and de Charis filed a claim with the Commission Against Piracy in Cornwall. They were confident that the agency would do its best to stop the ruthless pirates and recover their ship, hopefully in one piece. Their confidence wavered when they discovered that the commissioner was none other than John Killigrew, one of Lady Mary's sons. Unsurprisingly, despite a thorough investigation the commissioner was unable to find the culprit or recover the ship.

Still incensed that they had been duped, de Orozo and de Charis doggedly pursued their complaint. They pushed it up through the chain of command to the highest level, where it eventually landed on the desk of Queen Elizabeth. Now, the queen was in a pickle. To quietly pay off some port officials was one thing; to steal a ship from an ally in peacetime was quite another! She could not ignore the overwhelming evidence against the Killigrew family, nor the fact that Lady Mary's own son had presided over her trial. To do so would make the queen look like a fool at best, and at worst provoke hostilities with the Hanseatic League. On the other hand, to prosecute Lady Mary meant losing a valuable source of income. Was there any way that she could balance both of her interests and keep the Hanseatic League and the Killigrew family as allies?

Lady Mary Killigrew and the two household servants who had joined her on the raid were put on trial for the crime of piracy. All three were convicted, jailed, and sentenced to hang for their crimes. The two servants, Hawkins and Kendall, were indeed executed, but Lady Mary received a pardon from on high, possibly from Queen Elizabeth herself, and was sentenced to time served in 1585. She returned home to Arwenack Manor a free woman.

If Queen Elizabeth did issue the pardon, she likely did so in grateful recognition for the Killigrews's pirating services in the past, and in hope that the family would remain available for the queen's use in the future. With the conviction and pardon, she would have been able to avoid a war with the Hanseatic League and retain the Killigrews's financial aid. Her wisdom saved Lady Mary's life and England's prosperous future.

After her release from prison, Lady Mary Killigrew disappeared from the headlines. She most likely returned to the life of the gentlewoman she so often was when she wasn't pirating. In her life, she wielded many types of power: both the subtle powers of wealth and societal position and the brute powers of force and the sword. Was she more at home in her parlor pouring tea or on deck slashing throats? The world may never know.

Mary Killigrew's story is an excellent illustration of the many different types of power a woman can wield and how to work those powers to her best advantage.

Learn More

Druett, Joan. *She Captains: Heroines and Hellions of the Sea*. New York: Simon and Schuster, 2000.

Gosse, Phillip. *The History of Piracy*. Lt. ed. Mineola, NY: Dover, 2007.

Maria Cobham

An old saying claims that "absolute power corrupts absolutely." Maria Cobham never got close to absolute power, but she was definitely corrupt. While many pirates killed out of necessity or in self-defense, Maria Cobham killed for fun. She used the power that she gained during her lifetime to torture, humiliate, and kill her victims.

How did Maria become so sadistic? If she had remained on land, would she have eventually started murdering her clients, or was it the exposure to the sea and to pirate power that unleashed her darker side? Power is not good or evil on its own; what is done with power determines its nature. Maria Cobham is a clear example of a powerful woman who took every advantage of her might to indulge in her greatest pleasure. Her pleasure may not look like others' pleasure, but her pursuit of it, at least, is impressive.

Maria Cobham was born Maria Lindsey in England around 1700. Her family and childhood circumstances are unknown. She entered history as a young prostitute working in Plymouth Harbor, a busy harbor in the south of England located on the English Channel. One hundred years before Maria's time, the *Mayflower* sailed from there to the New World in search of religious freedom. In the early 1700s, the waters were teeming with pirates, not pilgrims.

One pirate, Eric Cobham, made a stop in Plymouth Harbor that would change the course of his life. Fresh from a voyage where he'd stolen thousands of pounds of gold, he met the young Maria in a tavern. He wooed her with stories of his foul life full of thievery, murder, and deceit. His gory tales of the business of pirating enchanted Maria instead of scaring her away. She was so impressed with his stories of murder and mayhem that when his ship left Plymouth Harbor a few days later, she was onboard with him.

Maria and Eric's marriage was most likely a "fleet marriage," a popular custom at the time that allowed people to get married without all the hassle of a traditional marriage. In Maria's time, a legal marriage required official licenses and announcements. There was no such thing as a courthouse marriage because every wedding happened through the church. Fleet marriages, on the other hand, were conducted inside Fleet Prison, which claimed to be beyond the church's rule. There were enough ordained ministers, both imprisoned there and living in the dangerous area surrounding the prison, who were willing to bend the rules . . . for a price. A filthy prison full of leering inmates instead of bridesmaids and a felon instead of a minister does not seem to be part of a dream wedding, but desperate times called for desperate measures. Besides, Maria did not seem like a sentimental girl who wanted a frilly, white wedding anyway.

Women, as a rule, were not welcome on ships, and Eric's ship was no exception. Eric's fellow crew members were not happy about their newest passenger, and some began demanding that Maria be left at the nearest port. Maria did not worry about the hostility toward her. She knew if she could not make the crew like her, then at least they would respect—or fear—her. To do that, she quickly became the cruelest pirate of them all. She was perfectly willing to plunge her dagger into a man's heart without a moment's hesitation.

Pirate stories are seldom without violence, but legends of Maria's bloodthirstiness are extreme, even for a pirate. She enjoyed stabbing people in the heart, tying people to the mast and using them for target practice, and sewing living people into bags and dumping them overboard, among other grisly methods of execution. Most stories about Maria do not center on the treasure she captured or her fighting skills; they focus on her love of torture and murder.

One of the most popular stories about Maria involves the capture of the Flemish brig the *Altona*. It was early in Maria's career when she and her crew captured the ship.

Maria decided she really liked the ship captain's uniform. Since she wanted it, she was going to have it. In front of the *Altona* crew and her own, she made the captain strip naked on deck. After he was completely humiliated, she shot him (and two of his crew members, just for fun). She then dressed in the now-ownerless uniform and promoted herself to first officer of the pirates. With that daring act of cruelty, her transformation from "Eric's woman" to crewmate was complete. From that moment on, she wore the uniform at all times. She even had copies of it made so that she always had a spare onboard if hers was ever bloodied or slashed beyond repair. After that episode, nobody dared to question Maria's authority. The other pirates were too terrified of her.

Ironically, just as Maria was beginning to learn how to exercise her power, her husband was growing tired of his own power. The swaggering pirate who had won his bride with gory stories was gone, replaced with a man who yearned for a quiet, respectable life on land. Twenty years on the sea was enough for him, and he was ready to retire.

Maria was not at all interested in giving up the pirate's life, but she eventually agreed to follow her husband ashore. Her one condition was that she wanted to live in a big house by the water. The estate she desired was 20 miles long and located on the coast of Le Havre, France. It was previously owned by the Duke of Chartres. To pay for it, the couple would have to capture one last heavily loaded pirate ship. Maria Cobham would not leave piracy quietly—she would go out with a bang, or not at all.

The couple waited until just the right prize came along. They listened for rumors of a big ship, finally choosing an East India Trading Company ship called the *Middleton* as their last target. It was large enough to meet their needs, if they were able to pull off the capture of the ship. But how would they do it?

Getting away with it would mean disposing of the entire crew. After all, dead men tell no tales. Maria had no problem with murder, but would she be able to commit mass murder? All accounts agree: yes, she would. Just how she did it, though, is the subject of a few different stories.

One account says that to secure her future, Maria locked the entire crew in chains and threw them overboard, alive. The unlucky sailors drowned as they sunk to the bottom of the sea, unable to swim to safety.

Another story is a bit more gruesome, but it seems like something that Maria might have enjoyed. It explains that the captured crew, no doubt aware of Maria's reputation for cruelty, was shocked when rather than immediately kill them, she served them a fine dinner and sent them down below to get some rest. Later that night, the whole ship rang out with the groans of the crew as they died slow and painful deaths from the poison that Maria had added to the food. The sun rose on a ship full of corpses, which Maria dumped overboard.

Whichever story is true, Maria made sure that nobody would be around to tell the truth about who stole the *Middleton.*

POISON: THE WOMAN'S TOOL?

History and popular culture are full of stories of woman poisoners. Poison was even called "the woman's weapon" by a depiction of Sherlock Holmes, the famous fictional detective. But how true is this stereotype?

The US Department of Justice reports that during a 28-year period, 60.5 percent of poisoners were male, while 39.5 percent were female. However, that same report found that murderers are 89.5 percent male and 10.5 percent female. So, while there are more male poisoners than female poisoners, there are more male murderers overall. Put another way, not all poisoners were women, but many women murderers are poisoners. Why might this be true?

There are many practical reasons. First, poison is usually administered in food or other medicines. Traditionally, women have been tasked with making and serving food. They typically have greater access to food while it cooks and so greater opportunity to add poison. Also, many household chemicals contain poisonous substances. So women, who often do most household shopping and cleaning, could buy poison without causing suspicion. There are, besides these practical reasons, personal ones as well. For example, women in history were virtually unable to obtain a divorce, even from an abusive husband. Murder was seen as the only escape, and poisoning was easier than prevailing in a contest of brute force.

In addition to Maria Cobham, there are several famous women poisoners. One, Lucrezia Borgia of Renaissance Italy, was said to wear a hollow ring in which she hid her poison. She has long been held up as the poster girl for poison, but recent scholarship suggests that she never poisoned anyone and was a victim of her family's bad reputation and her political enemies.

England's Mary Ann Cotton poisoned at least 20 people in the 1800s, most of whom were her own husbands and children. Nannie Doss was an American poisoner in the 1920s who confessed to killing eight people, four of them her husbands. Newspapers dubbed her the "Giggling Granny" because she often laughed while recounting her murders to the police.

The *Middleton* prize made the Cobhams a lot of money. Once they sold their own ship as well, they had more than enough to purchase Maria's dream home in Le Havre, a busy port where the River Seine and the English Channel meet. In Maria's time, a number of ships came through the port daily. Many wealthy traders chose this spot to build their homes so they could be close to the hustle and bustle of nautical life. It was a place for the rich and powerful—even King Louis XV visited the area in 1749. Maria and Eric resolved to enjoy their new life at the seaside.

Eric, at least, did embrace landlubbing life. He got involved in local politics and even became a magistrate judge. Life as a law-abiding citizen suited him, and he became a respected member of their new community. Sure, now and again he took the family yacht out for some minor pirating, but for the most part he was done with his life of crime. Never again did he do the big money and mass murder jobs he and Maria used to do. The couple settled down in their lovely home and had three children. By all appearances, the Cobham family was a perfectly normal and happy one.

But underneath the couple's polished surface, there were cracks. Maria did not adjust to lawful life on land as well as her husband did. She became a recluse, hiding out on the family estate. Occasionally she could be coaxed onto the yacht for a brief trip, but other than that, she rarely left home. Her family's attempts to reach her emotionally failed. Finally, after years of her self-imposed exile, Maria met her end.

How did Maria Cobham, expert killer, die? As usual, there are a number of theories but no conclusive proof. Pirate historian Philip Gosse reports that she took a fatal dose of laudanum, a drug used to help people sleep. Gosse claims that she was filled with shame for her life-time of wicked deeds and killed herself. Other sources suggest that she told Eric she was going for a walk along the cliffs and never returned home, leaving no trace of her whereabouts except a shawl washed up on the beach. Did she jump? Did she slip and fall? Did she run off with a lover and stage her own death? Any of these stories are possibly true. Yet another source, Howard Pyle's *Book of Pirates*, says that Eric was fed up with his wife's behavior and murdered her. Was she a victim of a tragic accident, a foul murder, or her own hand? The world will likely never know.

Maria's twisted tale has, fittingly, a twist ending. According to legend, Eric, overcome with guilt over his wife's death (whether he killed her or not) went to a priest to unburden himself of the long and sordid story of their past. During the last few years of his life, Eric told the priest everything that he and his wife had done. As he lay dying, he summoned the priest to perform last rites and hear his final confession. He handed over an account he had written about his and Maria's past, detailing over 20 years of pirating life. Eric made the priest promise to publish the account after his death so that the world would know what kind of a man he was. The priest, according to the story, kept his promise.

Why isn't this book in every bookstore in the world? Well, Eric and Maria's grown children were shocked when they learned what their parents had been up to before they were born. They knew that their lives in the high society of Le Havre were in major trouble if the story got out. They were determined to avoid a scandal at all cost, so they used their money and influence to make sure that every copy of the dangerous pamphlet disappeared. They were successful—save one copy that survived. The last copy is said to be tucked away in the archives of France. It is so well hidden that it has not yet been found. Somewhere on a dusty shelf in a dark basement, the truth about Maria Cobham still lies, waiting to be discovered.

The line between morally questionable and morally wrong is constantly changing as society and culture evolve. Pirates live to straddle that line. Maria Cobham is a good example of a woman who loved pushing the boundaries. No matter what the reader thinks of her methods, it is impossible to deny that she had great success in her pirating career. She entered piracy searching for power, and power she most certainly got.

Learn More

Gosse, Philip. *The Pirate's Who's Who.* New York: Burt Franklin, 1924.

Pyle, Howard. *Howard Pyle's Book of Pirates.* New York: Harper and Bros. Publishers, 1903.

Stanley, Jo, ed. *Bold in Her Breeches: Women Pirates Across the Ages.* London: Pandora Press, 1996.

Grace O'Malley

Grace O'Malley is a celebrated figure in the songs and stories of her home country of Ireland. There, she is known as the Pirate Queen. Other pirates, like Cheng I Sao, were more successful. Other pirates, like Mary Read and Anne Bonny, were more chronicled during their lives. But Grace O'Malley's story is somehow the best loved by pirate enthusiasts and pirate novices alike. Why? Her life is a textbook of female power: how to inherit it, how to capture it, and how to use it to your best advantage. Grace O'Malley went up against Queen Elizabeth I, and she won. Her power, like Queen Elizabeth's, is undeniable.

Even though she would spend her life on the sea, Grace O'Malley was born on land, most likely County Mayo, Ireland, around 1530. Most of her childhood was spent on small Clare Island in Clew Bay, where her family's castle stood. Her father, Dudara O'Malley, was the head of their clan. The O'Malleys were well-off fishers and sailors who occasionally got involved in some less-than-legal but profitable sailing and trading. From a young age, Gráinne—which has been anglicized to Grace—showed both the desire and the skill to join her father out to sea.

In Grace's time, it would have been unheard of for a daughter to follow in her father's footsteps instead of her mother's. Grace was a woman, and at that time it meant her destiny was cooking and childbearing, not seafaring and sword fighting.

ENGLAND AND IRELAND

The history between England and Ireland is long and complicated enough to fill entire books, and indeed many have been written. However, a brief summary is necessary to understand Grace's story.

Although soldiers fighting for the English crown first landed on Ireland's shores in the 1100s, England did not immediately take control of the country. English laws, language, and culture were confined to a small area around Dublin known as "the Pale." Everywhere else in Ireland, Gaelic laws, language, and culture were the rule. The two opposing sides did not have much in common and did not mix well. For example, England recognized a central government headed by a king or queen, while Ireland favored a clan system with bands of families such as the Burkes and the Fitzgeralds governing themselves across Ireland's land.

Irish culture was a mix of Catholic and older druid religion, while English culture was, in Henry VIII's time, Protestant. Ireland maintained control of itself until 1542, when Henry VIII (Queen Elizabeth I's father) was declared king of Ireland by the Irish Parliament. The Tudor takeover of Ireland was his (and his daughter's) plan to fully assert English control over all of Ireland. It was a long, bloody process that cost many lives and brewed much hatred between the two sides.

In Grace's time, England had not yet fully won the country (which it would hold until Ireland became a free state in 1922) and the whole of Ireland was in upheaval, uncertain of its future. Grace's career was a result of this tumultuous period in Ireland's history because she used the turbulent political situation to her advantage.

Grace was able, due to a combination of the uneasy state of Irish politics and her own persistence, to join her father at sea. According to the story, when she was told that she could not sail with her father because she was a girl, young Grace chopped off all of her hair and disguised herself as a boy. She tricked her way onto her father's crew and earned the nickname Granuaile, which is Gaelic for "Bald Grace." Her father cautioned her that the sea was dangerous for anyone, boy or girl. She would need to become a strong sailor and a brave one to survive Ireland's dangerous waters and rocky coastline.

Grace took his suggestions to heart because she proved herself many times, both on the sea and off. One story tells of a family of bald eagles that were terrorizing the O'Malley family's livestock. Young Grace, barely taller than the eagles, took to the fields to attack the birds and rescue her family's animals. She killed some of them and scared the rest away, but she did not escape the battle unharmed. One eagle sunk its talons into her forehead, leaving her with large and ugly scars that she would bear for the rest of her life.

Aboard her father's ship, she also demonstrated great bravery and strength. Once during an English attack on their ship, Grace was sent below decks and ordered to stay there, out of trouble. She watched the battle through the hatch, more fascinated than frightened. When she saw that her father needed help, she disobeyed his order and dashed into the middle of the battle, screaming fiercely and leaping onto the back of her father's attacker. She beat the man savagely and saved her father's life.

A childhood filled with so many wild adventures seemed destined for an exciting adulthood, but Grace was, above all, still the daughter of a chieftain and she had duties to fulfill on land. At age 16, her father arranged her marriage to Donal O'Flaherty, a political ally who was heir to the chieftainship in his own clan. The O'Flahertys were a rowdy clan, to put it mildly. Their love of brawling and pillaging was so well known that it was common to hear this refrain in the local churches: "From the ferocious O'Flahertys, the Good Lord deliver us." Grace, with her fiery spirit, was probably not intimidated by her husband's untamed nature and was likely as good a match as he could have hoped for. She and Donal had three children together, two sons and a daughter.

Donal had a nickname, Donal of the Battles. It was a well-earned nickname because he loved to fight. He loved to fight so much, in fact, that he waged battles when he should have been doing other things, like planting crops or governing his clan. Under his leadership, the O'Flahertys were starving. They asked Donal for help and he ignored them, so they turned to his wife. Grace was in a tough spot, because legally she could not take over her husband's duties as chieftain. However, she refused to let her adopted people starve if she could fix their situation. Grace unofficially took over the nonfighting parts of the chieftainship, including resource allocation for food. Once Grace got involved, people were again well fed. The O'Flaherty clan could never acknowledge Grace as their true leader in name, but they knew that in spirit she was responsible for them in a way that her husband was not.

Grace and Donal may have eventually fought over the fact that she had usurped much of his work as the chieftain, but Donal died before the argument had a chance to develop. Donal's death came during battle, which is no surprise. He had led his men into the fight to capture a castle that had once belonged to their clan but had since fallen to an enemy clan. The castle, Cock's Castle, was an island fortress. When Donal was slain, his troops prepared to retreat and give up the castle for good. Instead, they were rallied by Grace, who led them back to the castle and helped them capture it. She fought with such bravery and ferocity that Donal's men rechristened the castle Hen's Castle in her honor.

Grace had shown the clan that she was a strong and capable leader in both war and peacetime. However, the law prevented her from becoming the official chieftain in her husband's place after his death. A cousin of Donal's was chosen to replace him instead. Grace refused to meekly take on the role of widow when she had been so good at the role of chieftain. She decided that she was through with the rough O'Flaherty clan and with taking orders from other people. From now on, Grace would be ruled by nobody but herself.

Grace returned home to Clare Island with a group of O'Flaherty men who chose to serve her rather than Donal's replacement. When she returned to her family's land, she gathered more men around her, close to 200 of them. She selected men who were loyal, skilled, and strong—men who would serve her well on the high seas. Grace took a few of her father's old ships, put her crews on board, and sailed away from Clew Bay. Her old life was officially over. She was no longer Grace O'Flaherty, the widow, but Grace O'Malley, the pirate.

It didn't take Grace long to become successful at her new trade. Her childhood spent aboard her father's ship gave her excellent sailing skills and an incredible knowledge of the Irish coastline. Like many pirates before her, Grace used the geography of her homeland to hide from her victims and to escape them once she'd stolen what she wanted. English, Scottish, and other European ships didn't stand a chance of following her into the maze of small islands and rocky coves along the coast. Maps of Grace's Ireland did not exist. Even if her pursuers had known where to go to follow her, her faster and more maneuverable galley ships could sail through shallower waters and fit into smaller caves and coves than theirs could. Nobody could find her, and nobody could stop her. Grace gained the reputation of the Pirate Queen, with fiery red hair and a blazing spirit to match.

In the middle of all her pirating, Grace found time to marry a second time—again for strategic reasons—but this time it was her choice, not her father's. The man Grace chose was Richard Bourke (also spelled Burke), a Connacht chieftain who was in line for the MacWilliamship, the most powerful ruling office in the region. He owned a large fleet of trading ships and, most important to Grace, Rockfleet Castle. The fortress was a better place to shelter her fleet and crews than her current home base in Clew Bay. If Grace married Richard, she could get her hands on the castle. According to the story, Grace married Richard "for one year certain," an odd convention from ancient Brehon law. Under this law, during the first year of the marriage either party could withdraw if he or she chose. The marriage would then be considered officially annulled, as if it had never taken place.

Grace waited until she was confident that she could control the castle and then sent Richard on an errand outside the walls. As he rode home, she locked the castle gates and shouted at him from the battlements, "Richard Bourke, I dismiss you!" This was enough to end their marriage, but Richard and Grace remained friends and business partners. They often told people they were husband and wife, and even had a son together, Tibbott-ne-long.

BREHON LAW

Life in Ireland was once governed by Brehon law, an ancient civil code even older than the Celtic language. As a civil code, it was not concerned with criminal matters but instead civil matters like inheritance, property, and marriage. It began as an exclusively oral tradition, passed down from generation to generation from memory without the help of a written language. Eventually, however, it was written down.

Over the centuries, Brehon law mingled with Christian doctrine and adapted somewhat to suit the changing times. Modern scholars have called it progressive in its treatment of women, with some even claiming it prescribed near equality between the sexes. The law was extremely popular in the Middle Ages, but by the time of Grace O'Malley's life, it had almost completely been wiped out by English laws. The "one-year certain" marriage was one of the last remaining laws in practice during her lifetime.

Tibbott's birth was an important part of Grace's story for more than one reason. Tibbott was born at sea, which is why Grace named him Tibbott-ne-long (Theobald or Toby "of the Ships"). The day after he was born, their ship was attacked by Algerian corsairs. Without her, Grace's men were having a difficult time keeping the ship safe, and so they called for her to join them. Still recovering from giving birth, Grace cursed at them, muttering, "May you be seven times worse in one year, seeing you can't manage for even one day without me," and rose to join the battle. Her ragged appearance so surprised the corsairs that Grace was able to turn the tide of the battle. She fought the corsairs, saved the ship, and returned to bed, presumably grumbling all the while.

In 1577, Grace was imprisoned for the first time. She was captured by the Earl of Desmond when she was raiding his land and was sent to Dublin Castle. She served time there for 18 months but was eventually released as part of a plan to pacify Richard Bourke, who was plotting his own rebellion. This plan backfired because after her release, Richard and Grace remained as rebellious (and as piratical) as they ever were.

Grace nearly met her match in Richard Bingham, sent as a new governor to Ireland at Queen Elizabeth's request. He arrived in England in 1583, which was the same year that Richard Bourke died. Bingham was part of Queen Elizabeth's plan to mold the Irish chieftains and their people into proper, submissive English subjects. He was ruthless and cunning, and he particularly hated Grace O'Malley and the Irish freedom spirit for which she stood.

Grace hated Bingham as much as he hated her. She conducted three separate rebellion plots against him before she was captured by him. Bingham planned to execute her, but at the last minute she was saved by a chieftain of a neighboring clan who traded some other hostages for her life. The chieftain's act is proof of how respected Grace had become by this time, not just in her own clan but in many others as well.

But Bingham would not be denied his revenge on Grace. He confiscated much of her property, including her horse and cattle herds. He also kidnapped two of her sons, Owen O'Flaherty and Tibbott-ne-long. Owen, the older son, died while in Bingham's custody, possibly murdered by Bingham's men. When news of Owen's death reached her, Grace realized how serious Bingham was about hurting her. This time, there would be no last-minute rescue. To save her youngest son, Grace would have to appeal to someone with more authority than Bingham. She would have to appeal to a higher power— a fellow queen.

In 1593, Grace sent a letter directly to Queen Elizabeth asking for her son Tibbott's release. She did not lie about her pirate life, but she was smart enough to portray it in a sympathetic light. She claimed that circumstances had forced her to take up arms to protect her family and her people. If Elizabeth would release her son, Grace said that she would devote her life to sailing against the queen's enemies, answering only to Elizabeth herself. This proposition conveniently cut Bingham out of Grace's life. She sent her letter to England and waited anxiously for a reply.

Queen Elizabeth was intrigued by this woman who had appealed to her so boldly, despite her obvious past acts against England. She replied to Grace with a list of 18 questions, which Grace answered very carefully. She offered a rose-colored portrait of her life and career to the queen, showing herself to be a smart and remarkable woman. Meanwhile, Bingham upped the stakes and charged Tibbott with treason. If he was tried for this offense, he would almost certainly be hanged.

Grace had already lost one son to Bingham, and she would not lose another. In July 1593 she set sail for England, carrying with her the answers to the queen's questions. Grace intended to deliver them in person. This was an extremely bold move. England's ports were decorated with the rotting bodies of hanged criminals, many of them pirates. When Grace sailed to England, she knew she might join the collection of the executed criminals. But her love for Tibbott, and her way of life, was stronger than her love of her own life. She would bring Tibbott home or die trying.

Against Bingham's strenuous objections, the queen granted Grace an audience with her in the fall of 1593. Unfortunately, the details of what happened when queen met queen are lost to history. Legends abound about what they wore, what they said, and who was taller than whom. A woodcut from the time of the two queens is thought to depict their meeting, but only those present know for sure what happened. Many stories claim that the conversation took place in Latin since Grace spoke no English and Elizabeth spoke no Irish, but it is clear from her letters that Grace did in fact speak English, so they may well have spoken English at the meeting. Grace's boldness and Elizabeth's unique sense of humor must have made for a lively discussion. The two women—whose lives were starkly different but also so much the same—would certainly remember the encounter for the rest of their lives.

At the end of the meeting, Tibbott was freed and Grace was allowed to take him home. Grace was allowed to return to her pirating, this time with the queen's blessing. Bingham was instructed to provide Grace with a pension to maintain her once she retired from the sea, much to his outrage. He tried to protest and even disobeyed the queen by posting troops on Grace's lands. For this, he was eventually called back to England in disgrace. He had no place in the story of these two women. Grace and Elizabeth made it to the top of a man's world and became leaders of their people. When they came together, they were able to use their power to, for a moment, set the world right.

Grace died in 1603—the same year as Queen Elizabeth. She died of old age, at home, in her beloved Rockfleet Castle. She is said to be buried on Clare Island where she grew up, at an abbey with a view of the sea. Though she died over 400 years ago, the stories of her power live on. She is an eternal reminder that every woman can, when needed, summon enormous power. Grace's bravery gave her the power to follow the path she truly wanted—out to sea. Her compassion gave her the power to rule the O'Flahertys when her husband would not. Her intelligence gave her the power to seize Rockfleet Castle and make a lifelong ally of its owner. Her love for her son gave her the power to go toe-to-toe with a queen and leave with what she wanted. It is all of this power that made her the beloved pirate that she remains today.

Learn More

Chambers, Anne. *Granuaile: Grace O'Malley, Ireland's Pirate Queen*. Rev. ed. Dublin: Gill & MacMillan, 2009.

Ronald, Susan. *The Pirate Queen: Queen Elizabeth I, Her Pirate Adventurers, and the Dawn of an Empire*. 1st American ed. New York: Harper, 2007.

Sjoholm, Barbara. *The Pirate Queen: In Search of Grace O'Malley and Other Legendary Women of the Sea*. New York: Seal Press, 2004.

Cheng I Sao

What does it mean to be successful as a pirate? Having the biggest ships and the largest crew? Making the most money? Or remaining alive and out of jail the longest?

No matter which metric is used to define success, Cheng I Sao met them all. She had a fleet of around a thousand ships and somewhere between 40,000 and 60,000 pirates under her command—larger than many legitimate navies of the time. During her nearly 10-year career, she amassed uncounted wealth, took on the Chinese navy and won, and struck fear into the hearts of sailors all over the South China Sea. Cheng I Sao was the most successful pirate of all time, male or female. She was not born into power, but she seized it every chance she got and used it to build the most impressive pirate empire the world has ever seen.

THE QING DYNASTY

Cheng I Sao grew up during the Qing dynasty, China's last dynasty. For thousands of years, China was ruled by emperors. These emperors were believed to have been given the mandate of heaven, which is a blessing bestowed by heaven on a just and worthy ruler and passed down through the family. When a ruling family lost the mandate, a new family would be chosen by heaven and a new dynasty would rise. The dynasty system lasted in China from 2070 BCE to 1912 CE, when China became a republic.

The Qing dynasty, started in 1644, was ruled by the Manchu family. It was a period of great change. At first, China grew and prospered. Until the end of the 18th century, things were going very well. But after Emperor Qianlong's reign, things began to go downhill. Population exploded, and the government was not nimble enough to keep up with the growing needs of its people. As European countries stabilized and solidified, they began to put pressure on China to compete. Corruption crept into the government ranks, breeding unrest among the people, who were unhappy with government waste spreading while the common people were starving. Finally, the opium wars with England drove nails in the coffin of the Qing dynasty. When Emperor Pu Yi abdicated in 1912, he brought an end to the Qing dynasty and over 5,000 years of dynastic rule in China.

Few details of Cheng I Sao's early life are known, including her real name. Cheng I Sao means "wife of Cheng I." She was probably born in modern-day Canton around 1775. Canton is a seaside city, so Cheng I Sao would have grown up learning the rhythms of maritime life—how the currents worked, where the merchant ships were coming from and heading toward, and where the best fish could be found.

Cheng I Sao eventually found employment on a "flower boat," which is a floating brothel. The local government had strict rules about outsiders coming onto Chinese land, so strangers had to obtain the services of prostitutes on the water. One of her customers was Cheng I, a small-time pirate with big aspirations. There are many legends about how the pair met, how Cheng I proposed, and how she responded to his proposal, but the only thing that is certain is that the pair eventually wed in 1801.

THE OPIUM WARS

Cheng I Sao rose to prominence in a China much weakened by war—war that was, in a way, started over tea. In the 1800s, England was absolutely wild for Chinese tea. It was exported to Europe by the trunkful, making the Chinese very wealthy. The English were unhappy with the unequal trade situation since they had nothing of equal necessity to offer the Chinese.

Eventually the English found a solution: opium. Their introduction of this drug into China caused two wars, brought down a dynasty, and opened the once-isolated China to the rest of the world. It also ruined the lives of countless Chinese citizens who became addicted to it.

Opium is a drug extracted from the poppy flower. It has been used in various forms since ancient times. Modern drugs such as heroin, as well as legal medicines such as codeine and morphine, all come from the opium poppy. The drug makes its user feel pleasant and drowsy, but it is fiercely addictive.

Opium was banned in China by the mid-18th century, but traders found ways to smuggle it in. By 1838, 40,000 chests were imported annually. The political and economic instability that resulted from the opium wars, as well as from the opium trade, had considerably damaged China.

Instead of a honeymoon, the newlyweds took a trip to present-day Vietnam to help out during the Tay Son rebellion. The Tay Son leaders paid Chinese pirates to fill the ranks of their small fighting force. In Vietnam the Chinese pirates, including Cheng I and his wife, learned a valuable lesson, despite the fact that the Tay Son rebellion was ultimately unsuccessful. They discovered that one ship at a time, they did not pose much of a threat to their opponents, but when they worked together they become stronger and more dangerous. The lessons learned in Vietnam would serve as a blueprint for the Cheng family's strategy going forward. They would unite the ragtag pirates of the South China Sea and become a force to be reckoned with.

It took Cheng I about four years to unify his fleet. He and his wife worked hard to bring the formerly warring pirates together into a strong confederation. He built a fleet with himself at the head, divided up under seven pirate captains who reported to him. Each fleet flew a different colored flag that gave the fleet its name: Red Flag Fleet, Blue Flag Fleet, Black Flag Fleet, and so on.

From 1805 to 1807, the couple ran a powerful operation. They continually added more ships and pirates to the fleet, as well as more treasure to the chests. But in 1807, Cheng I died suddenly, either in battle or from being washed overboard. His death threatened to collapse the entire pirate empire that he and his wife had built. For the fleet to remain stable, a powerful commander would have to step up and fill Cheng I's shoes. The fleet required a strong commander whom it trusted with their lives. That commander turned out to be none other than Cheng I Sao, the late commander's wife.

For a woman to take over her husband's job after his death was not entirely unprecedented. In this era of Chinese culture, men and women often sailed together on fishing and trading boats. What was unprecedented was how large of a job it was, how much was at stake, and how well Cheng I Sao would do with the empire she'd been left. Her husband had been a good pirate manager; she was a magnificent one. Under her leadership, the

fleet grew by leaps and bounds and business was boom-
ing. She had to establish accounting offices on land to
keep track of how much money was coming in—that's
how well the fleet was doing financially. Where most
pirates spent their treasure as quickly as they received it,
Cheng I Sao had to build banks.

To ensure that her word was law in the fleet, Cheng
I Sao appointed a new captain of the Red Flag Fleet, her
largest and most powerful fleet. Chang Pao, her adopted
son, would absolutely obey her and immediately inform
her if one of the other captains was considering disloyalty
or somehow running afoul of her wishes. He was a promising sailor whom her late husband had groomed to be his
successor and adopted to establish the all-important family connection necessary for business relations in China.
Cheng I Sao went one step further in securing his loyalty
and compliance: she married Chang Pao. Whether she
decided to do this for love, power, or some other reason
altogether, only she knew for sure. Cheng I Sao remained
at the top of the fleet, as she was before Cheng I's death,
only now she had a new husband by her side.

Cheng I Sao's operation was so massive that she
needed complete obedience among her sailors to keep it
running smoothly. She created a code of conduct to give
her sailors rules to live by and punishments if they disobeyed. It was an impressive code that served to make
her reputation loom even larger than it did already.

Many pirates had codes of conduct. Bartholomew
Roberts had a particularly strict one, for example, but

Cheng I Sao's was remarkable for both the harshness of its penalties and the severity with which rape was punished. Men could choose a woman from their female captives, but he had to marry her and remain faithful to her, upon pain of death. Rape was punishable by death also. People captured by Cheng I Sao later said that her code was well known throughout the fleet and strictly enforced. If a sailor disobeyed Cheng I Sao, he was most likely going to meet his end.

Besides actual pirating, Cheng I Sao organized a protection racket that brought in additional money. The size and strength of her fleet left much of the Chinese coast unguarded, as the Chinese navy was too afraid to go after her. She was able to charge fees to fishermen and merchant sailors to protect them from other pirates (as well as her own). If a ship under her protection were attacked, she paid restitution for the loss or damage. This scheme provided the means that kept her pirate fleet running. The day-to-day expenses of supporting 50,000 men would have been staggering, not to mention the cost for upkeep of the ships. Cheng I Sao's plan to collect protection money kept her fleet afloat, literally and figuratively. Where other pirates would have quickly grown their fleets too large to sustain and run out of money, Cheng I Sao's financial savvy allowed her to continually expand her operations.

Obviously, the Chinese navy was not happy with her. This woman was the terror of the South China Sea, taking whatever she wanted, whenever she wanted. They tried many times to fight her, but she beat them every time. China at this time was very isolationist and hated dealing with other countries, but it was forced to do the thing it least wanted to do: ask for help abroad. First Portugal, and then Britain, sent warships, but neither nation's contribution was able to deal a killing blow to Cheng I Sao's pirates. She had, in effect, built her own state, and it was too powerful to be taken down by anyone.

Tales of her pirates' brutality ran rampant through the rumor mill. If Cheng I Sao killed her own crew members with impunity for breaking her rules, the Chinese reasoned, what on earth would she do to her enemies? Stories spread of some captives being nailed to the deck and beaten, or dismembered. There were frequent references to her crew hacking people into small pieces. Kwo Lang, a Chinese admiral, committed suicide after losing to Cheng I Sao in battle rather than risk being captured by her pirates. And he was not the only man to do so.

Cheng I Sao, while she was in charge, was so good at her job that some people believed she was magic. Eyewitnesses from aboard her ships reported that she sprinkled her captives with garlic water, which was said to be a charm against gunshot wounds. She also was said to have a statue of a god on her ship, which she consulted before making any major moves. With the success she had, it was not hard to believe that she was in league with supernatural forces.

In 1808, Cheng I Sao's fleet wiped out roughly half

of the Chinese navy. In 1809, the Chinese decided they had lost enough. They mustered every resource they had and forced Cheng I Sao into a narrow channel. It appeared that, for the moment, they had her trapped. Officials came from all over China to finally witness the end of this fearsome pirate who had plagued them for so long. For eight days, November 20–28, 1809, the Chinese fired on Cheng I Sao. Although she was clearly trapped, she did not offer to surrender.

After the eight long days of constant firing, the Chinese seemed to be at a stalemate. They did not want to sail closer to Cheng I Sao's ships and engage them in hand-to-hand combat, nor did they want her to get away. They decided to up the stakes by sending in fireships. A fireship is a ship that has been set on fire, sailed directly into an enemy's line to set *their* ships on fire, and generally set their ships into panic. But the eight fireships did not cause panic in Cheng I Sao's fleet. After she successfully sunk one of them by firing on it, the wind shifted and sent the other seven back toward the Chinese fleet. They scattered, and Cheng I Sao and her pirates were able to slip away, hungry and exhausted after more than a week of cannon fire, but alive and unharmed. It seemed that no force on the planet could stop Cheng I Sao.

Most pirates left the profession at the end of a noose or the business end of a cannon. Not Cheng I Sao. In 1810, discord was brewing among her various fleets. Cheng I Sao, ever the shrewd businesswoman, knew that things could not continue to operate forever as smoothly as they had been. She decided that she would go out of the pirate game her way—on top, and with the government's blessing. Chang Pao was sent to negotiate a surrender with the government, but negotiations broke down before an agreement could be reached and he returned to her empty-handed.

Cheng I Sao realized that to pull of the biggest surrender in the history of piracy, she would have to do it herself. She thought carefully about how to proceed. What she was attempting to do had never been done before. As she had so many times before, she was going to have to make her own rules.

Cheng I Sao assembled a team of women and children to accompany her to the negotiations. They went in unarmed, which was a brilliant move that surprised her enemies and shifted the balance of power even more to her favor. She came to the table knowing she could ask for whatever she wanted and, obviously, the Chinese would have no choice but to accept. She filled her surrender document full of language that was respectful and polite to the Chinese government, asking its pardon for the pirates' wicked ways. It is possible, even likely, that she was mocking the government, given that she had no real need to surrender, nor did the government have the means to fight her if she were anything other than the obedient servant of a wise and powerful government.

Whatever the reason, her apologetic language worked. She walked away from the surrender with a small fleet for her own private use; a good government job for her husband, Chang Pao; her own treasure; and amnesty for all but a few hundred of her thousands of pirates. Best of all, the government provided a fund to aid these pirates-turned-good-citizens in their transition to civilian life. So not only did her pirates escape the gallows, they also got a check from the government when they retired.

By all measures, this surrender was a tremendous success. Nowhere in pirate history had so many pirates peacefully transitioned out of piracy with so much of their money intact. Woodes Rogers's pirate-by-pirate pardon policy seems amateurish compared to this massive surrender. It was a crowning achievement for the queen of the pirates.

After her "retirement" from pirate life, Cheng I Sao lived out the rest of her days lawfully. Some accounts claim she started a casino and brothel of her own. Others say she lived a quiet life in the country. She died in 1844 at the age of 69—one of only a handful of pirates in this book to die of old age. Her incredible life story, from prostitute to powerful commander, demonstrates that the circumstances of one's birth do not define a person. With determination and hard work, not to mention a little bit of luck, anyone can be a success—and perhaps even the most successful of all time.

Learn More

Murray, Dian H. *Pirates of the South China Coast 1790–1810*. Stanford, CA: Stanford University Press, 1987.

Rowe, William T. *China's Last Empire: The Great Qing.* Reprint ed. Cambridge, MA: Harvard University Press, 2010.

Van Dyke, Paul. *The Canton Trade: Life and Enterprise on the China Coast, 1700–1845.* Hong Kong University Press, 2007.

Epilogue

The world needs female pirate stories. Hopefully this book has convinced you that history is not an immovable concept; it can change based on who is writing it down. What is said about a person is controlled by the person telling the story. When only white men are allowed to write about women, women are not portrayed as fully as they could be. This is even more true when the women are women of color or part of other minority groups. After all, how can you really explain what it is like to live someone's life unless you have walked a mile in their shoes?

There has never been a better time in history to be a woman than right now. Women all over the world are seizing their power, raising their voices, and refusing to back down. They are forcing the world to take notice of them and to work with them for a kinder, more just world. For tolerance and equality to continue to grow, stories must be *told* by the people the stories are *about*. This will not happen unless women and other groups that have long been silenced are allowed to tell their stories in their own way.

This will not be easy—support and inspiration will be needed to change the system. Who better to inspire these system-changers than pirate women? They are no strangers to breaking the rules and going after what they deserve, no matter what anyone else says. The pirate women in this book sailed fearlessly where no woman had ever been before. May we all be empowered to do the same.

Notes

Introduction

"*the past and history*": Keith Jenkins, *Re-thinking History* (New York: Routledge, 1993), 7.

Sayyida al-Hurra

"*the King of the Sea*": E. Hamilton Currey, R.N., *Sea-Wolves of the Mediterranean* (London: John Murray, 1910), 220.

"*undisputed leader of the pirates*": Fatima Mernissi, *Forgotten Queens of Islam* (Minneapolis, MN: University of Minnesota Press, 1993), 18.

Jeanne de Clisson

"*the courage of the man*": Jean Froissart, *Chroniques*, (Paris: Chez Jules Renouard, 1870), 114.

Lagertha

"*to conquer enemies*": Jo Stanley, *Bold in Her Breeches: Women Pirates Across the Ages* (London: Pandora Press, 1995), 78.

"fought in front": Saxo Grammaticus, *Gesta Danorum*, trans. Oliver Elton (Liberty, MO: Jotun's Bane Kindred, 2012), 317.

"gain the victory": Grammaticus, *Gesta Danorum*, 318.

"spurned his mission": Grammaticus, *Gesta Danorum*, 318.

"this most presumptuous dame": Grammaticus, *Gesta Danorum*, 320.

"skilled warrior with experience": Grammaticus, *Gesta Danorum*, 126.

"pursued and slew": Grammaticus, *Gesta Danorum*, 126.

"the souls of men": Grammaticus, *Gesta Danorum*, 277.

Alfhild

"beyond the valor": Grammaticus, *Gesta Danorum*, 253.

"fight with kisses": Grammaticus, *Gesta Danorum*, 254.

Margaret Jordan

"to the best of my knowledge": F. Murray Greenwood, *Uncertain Justice: Canadian Women and Capital Punishment, 1754–1953* (Toronto: Dundurn Press, 2000), 65.

Charlotte Badger

"enormously fat woman": Roy Alexander, "Australia's Only Woman Pirate," *Sydney Morning Herald*, October 26, 1937.

Mary Read

"enter'd herself on board": Daniel Defoe, *A General History of the Pyrates* (Mineola, NY: Dover Maritime, 1999), 154.

Artemisia

"my men have become": Herodotus, *Histories*, trans. George Rawlinson (New York: Everyman's Library, 1997), 8.88.

Teuta

"*kill the one*": Polybius, *Histories*, trans. W. R. Paton (Cambridge, MA: Harvard University Press, 2010), 83.

Rachel Wall

"*solemn warning and caution*": Rachel Wall, *Life, Last Words and Dying Confession, of Rachel Wall: Who, with William Smith and William Dunogan, Were Executed at Boston, on Thursday, October 8, 1789, for High-way Robbery* (Boston printed broadside).

Sadie Farrell

"*ramshackle tenements*": Herbert Asbury, *Gangs of New York: An Informal History of the Underworld* (New York: Vintage, 2008), 43.

"*more violent crime*": Asbury, *Gangs of New York*, 45.

"*The river pirates pursue*": Asbury, *Gangs of New York*, 68.

"*inspired leadership*" . . . "*her ruffianly followers*": Asbury, *Gangs of New York*, 59.

Anne Bonny

"*no time wasted*": Clinton V. Black, *Tales of Old Jamaica* (London: Collins, 1966), 71.

"*were very active on Board*": *The Tryals of John Rackham and the Pirates* (Jamaica: Robert Baldwin, 1721), 18.

"*[the women] were both*": *The Tryals of John Rackham*, 19.

"*two women, by name*": Woodes Rogers, "Proclamation of Jack Rackham and Others as Pirates," *Boston Gazette*, January 31, 1721.

"*sorry to see him there*": Defoe, *A General History of the Pyrates*, 165.

"*Piracies, Felonies, and Robberies*": *The Tryals of John Rackham*, 16.

Lady Mary Killigrew

"veritable oligarchy": Phillip Gosse, *The History of Piracy* (Mineola, NY: Dover, 2007), 107.

Grace O'Malley

"From the ferocious": Joan Druett, *She Captains: Heroines and Hellions of the Sea* (New York: Simon and Schuster, 2000), 54.

"for one year certain": Druett, *She Captains*, 58.

"Richard Bourke": Druett, *She Captains*, 58.

"May you be seven times": Druett, *She Captains*, 59.

Selected Bibliography

Asbury, Herbert. *Gangs of New York: An Informal History of the Underworld*. New York: Vintage, 2008.

Chambers, Anne. *Granuaile: Grace O'Malley, Ireland's Pirate Queen*. Rev. ed. Dublin: Gill & MacMillian, 2009.

Cordingly, David. *Seafaring Women: Adventures of Pirate Queens, Female Stowaways, and Sailors' Wives*. Reprint ed. New York: Random House, 2001.

Cordingly, David. *Under the Black Flag: The Romance and Reality of Life Among the Pirates*. New York: Random House, 2006.

Defoe, Daniel. *A General History of the Pyrates*. Mineola, New York: Dover Maritime, 1999. Previously published as Johnson, Captain Charles. *A General History of the Robberies and Murders of the Most Notorious Pyrates*. 1724.

Druett, Joan. *She Captains: Heroines and Hellions of the Sea*. New York: Simon and Schuster, 2000.

Gosse, Phillip. *The History of Piracy*. Lt. ed. Mineola, NY: Dover, 2007.

Grammaticus, Saxo. *Gesta Danorum*, trans. Oliver Elton. Liberty, MO: Jotun's Bane Kindred, 2012.

Klausmann, Ulrike et al. *Women Pirates and the Politics of the Jolly Roger*. Trans. Nicholas Levis. Montreal: Black Rose Books, 1997.

Konstam, Angus. *Piracy: The Complete History*. Oxford: General Military, 2008.

Mernissi, Fatima. *Forgotten Queens of Islam*. Minneapolis, MN: University of Minnesota Press, 1993.

Murray, Dian H. *Pirates of the South China Coast 1790–1810*. Stanford, CA: Stanford University Press, 1987.

Sherry, Frank. *Raiders and Rebels: The Golden Age of Piracy*. Reprint ed. New York: Harper Perennial, 2008.

Stanley, Jo, ed. *Bold in Her Breeches: Women Pirates Across the Ages*. London: Pandora Press, 1995.

Wilson, Peter Lamborn. *Pirate Utopias: Moorish Corsairs and European Renegadoes*. 2nd ed. Brooklyn, NY: Autonomedia, 2003.

Woodard, Colin. *Republic of Pirates: Being the True and Surprising Story of the Caribbean Pirates and the Man Who Brought Them Down*. Boston: Mariner Books, 2008.

Index